Exercise Book Empirical Economic Research and Econometrics

Peter Winker • Christoph Funk • Elena Tönjes

Exercise Book Empirical Economic Research and Econometrics

Springer Gabler

Peter Winker
Business Studies and Economics
Justus Liebig University Giessen
Giessen, Germany

Christoph Funk
Independent Researcher
Bonn, Nordrhein-Westfalen, Germany

Elena Tönjes
Independent Researcher
Staufenberg, Hessen, Germany

ISBN 978-3-662-72712-6 ISBN 978-3-662-72713-3 (eBook)
https://doi.org/10.1007/978-3-662-72713-3

Extended and updated translation from "Übungsbuch Empirische Wirtschaftsforschung und Ökonometrie" by Peter Winker et al., © Der/die Herausgeber bzw. der/die Autor(en), exklusiv lizenziert durch Springer-Verlag GmbH, DE, ein Teil von Springer Nature 2021. Published by Springer Berlin Heidelberg. All Rights Reserved.

This Springer imprint is published by the registered company Springer-Verlag GmbH, DE, part of Springer Nature.
The registered company address is: Heidelberger Platz 3, 14197 Berlin, Germany

Preface

More than 20 years ago, I published a German textbook on "Empirical Economic Research" covering both issues related to the data basis of applied economic research and basic econometric techniques used in this context. It has been updated in several editions and is used for courses at different universities as an introduction to applied economic research and econometrics. It got a companion book covering exercises of different types with an updated German edition 2021.

For several years, I also taught the corresponding course in English to international students. While there exist many excellent textbooks dealing with the often formally challenging aspects of econometric theory and some of the pitfalls of applied econometrics, it turned out to be more difficult to find options for practicing the applied perspective using closed and open exercise questions. Therefore, I decided to offer an English version closely following the latest German edition with a few extensions and minor updates. The translation was supported by AI tools, but the final review was done by myself. I hope the book will be useful to future generations of students who are following related courses in empirical economic research and applied econometrics.

Christoph Funk contributed to the first and second German editions of the exercise book, and Elena Tönjes contributed to the second edition. They share only the responsibility for the original German version of the exercises adopted one-to-one in the English version, but not for new exercises and the updates of existing ones.

I am indebted to former teaching assistants and PhD students who contributed to building this pool of questions, in particular, to Jenny Bethäuser, Virginie Blaess, Sebastian Bredl, Dania Eugenidis, Björn Fastrich, Henning Fischer, Iris Gönsch, Daniel Grabowski, Albina Latifi, Jochen Lüdering, Mark Meyer, Viktoriia Naboka-Krell, Jana Röder, Nicola Stork, and Dennis Türk. Special thanks go to Mikhail Vereshchagin for his organization of the translation of existing questions and his suggestions for some new exercises.

Nevertheless, the author is responsible for all errors in the exercises and possibly misleading sample solutions. Any constructive feedback on such errors and other omissions would be greatly appreciated for future improvements.

Giessen, Germany
October 2025

Peter Winker

Instructions for Use

Dear reader,

The original German version of this exercise book was developed as a supplement to my German textbook on "Empirical Economic Research and Econometrics." It is aimed at students, lecturers, and other interested readers who wish to deepen their knowledge by solving practical exercises. The numbering of sections in Chaps. 1 through 6 of the exercise book directly refers to the corresponding chapters of the textbook (Sect. 1.5, for example, provides multiple choice, true or false, and supplementary questions for Chap. 5, "Input-Output Analysis," of the textbook, while solutions to these questions are provided in Sect. 4.5).

To successfully complete the individual exercises, you should have gained a basic understanding of the concepts covered in these chapters. Given that there exists no English version of the textbook yet, you will have to collect this knowledge from attending lectures or reading other textbooks on applied economic research and introductory textbooks on econometrics with a rather applied focus.

Chapter 1 contains multiple choice, true or false, and completion questions. These are primarily intended to quickly test your understanding of the content of the individual chapters. However, some of these questions require more in-depth reasoning or even small calculations. Solutions to all of these questions can be found in Part II, Chap. 4.

Chapter 2 deals with exercises and exam questions for an in-depth study. These include calculation and comprehension questions as well as many practical examples that require the interpretation of outputs generated using econometric software such as Eviews or R. Detailed sample solutions for some of these problems can be found in the solutions Part II, Chap. 5.

Finally, Chap. 3 comprises exercises based on specific short texts. Therefore, before trying to answer these questions, it is required to read these text. This offers an opportunity to discuss the practical questions of empirical economic research in the context of scientific or economic policy-oriented texts. Regarding the sample solutions to these questions, it should be noted that evaluation of empirical research does often allow not just for one correct answer. Therefore, the comments provided in Chap. 6 should be considered as hints rather than as complete and definitive answers.

I hope you have a lot of fun and gain substantial and useful knowledge from working on exercises for different aspects of empirical economic research and econometrics.

Contents

Part I

Exercises

Multiple Choice Questions 1

In this chapter, you will find multiple choice, true or false, and fill-in-the-blank (completion) questions. The multiple-choice questions each have exactly one correct answer. The same applies to the true or false questions. For the completion questions, the missing term(s) should be entered in the designated space. You will find solutions to all the questions of this chapter in Chap. 4 and some additional comments for some selected exercises.

1.1 Tasks and Principles of Empirical Economic Research

1.1.1. Multiple Choice

Not an objective of empirical economic research is ...

(a) ... analyzing past developments to assess the quality of economic models. . ○
(b) ... adjusting the data to an existing model. . . . . ○
(c) ... forecasting future developments. . . . . ○
(d) ... quantifying model relationships. . . . . ○

1.1.2. Multiple Choice

No question that can be meaningfully addressed using empirical economic research methods is ...

(a) ... which industries were the most affected in their revenues by the nearly total suspension of air traffic in spring 2020. . . . . ○
(b) ... whether a five-tier income tax system is fairer than a three-tier system. . ○
(c) ... what labor market effects the introduction of a nationwide minimum wage would have. . . . . ○

P. Winker et al., *Exercise Book Empirical Economic Research and Econometrics*,
https://doi.org/10.1007/978-3-662-72713-3_1

(d) ... whether higher investments in education lead to higher long-term growth. ○

1.1.3. `Multiple Choice`

No question that can be meaningfully addressed using empirical economic research methods is ...

(a) ... which economic sectors are directly or indirectly particularly affected by a train driver strike. ○
(b) ... how strong the effects of a real exchange rate appreciation would be for German exporters if the Euro zone were to collapse. ○
(c) ... whether the increasing inequality in income distribution in Germany, as measured by an increasing Gini coefficient, is fair. ○
(d) ... whether higher education expenditures lead to higher long-term growth. ○

1.1.4. `Multiple Choice`

No question that can be meaningfully addressed using empirical economic research methods is ...

(a) ... whether a higher proportion of female executives increases company success. ○
(b) ... whether the expected earnings of economics graduates are higher than those of mathematics graduates. ○
(c) ... whether the brand value of a company's products has an impact on company profit. ○
(d) ... whether joint financing of unemployment insurance in Europe is fair. ○

1.1.5. `Multiple Choice`

Which of the following questions **cannot** be answered using only methods from empirical economic research?

(a) What is the effect of joint spousal tax declarations on income tax revenue? ○
(b) Does joint spousal tax declarations increase or decrease the inequality of the income distribution? ○
(c) How large is the effect of the option of joint spousal tax declarations on the labor supply of married people who primarily take on care tasks for children and or elderly? ○
(d) Is the option of joint spousal tax declarations still appropriate in view of an existing labor shortage? ○

1.1.6. `Multiple Choice`

The principle of empirical economic research is described as the interaction of theory and empiricism. Which of the following is **not** part of an analysis in the field of empirical economic research?

(a) A political assessment of the desired outcome. ○
(b) A well-founded theoretical model for the phenomena/relationships under consideration. ○

(c) Data to describe the phenomena under consideration. .... ○
(d) A statistical theory matching the model and data. .... ○

1.1.7. `Multiple Choice`
Oxfam International published a study in March 2017 titled "Opening the Vaults" on the taxation of European major banks (https://oi-files-d8-prod.s3.eu-west-2.amazonaws.com/s3fs-public/bp-opening-vaults-banks-tax-havens-270317-en_0.pdf). It shows that the relationship between the reported profit and the number of employees varies greatly. Particularly high ratios were found for the countries Luxembourg and Ireland.
Which of the following statements **cannot** be verified using empirical economic research methods alone?
(a) The profits per employee reported by the banks are negatively correlated with the tax rates of the respective country. .... ○
(b) The profits per employee reported by the banks negatively correlate with the tax rates of the respective country, when other influencing factors such as the volume of deposits and loans in the country are taken into account. .... ○
(c) The distribution of the reported profits by the banks across countries cannot be modeled solely by the volume of deposits and loans and the number of employees. .... ○
(d) The banks are acting unethically by systematically shifting profits to countries with low tax rates. .... ○

1.1.8. `Multiple Choice`
When considering households that only receive income from basic security benefits for employment seekers according to SGB II ("Hartz IV"), there are various topics that are politically debated. Using empirical economic research methods alone **cannot** determine ...
(a) ... whether the price development for the products purchased by these households differs from the general price development of the consumer. ....○
(b) ... whether the household income, considering household size and composition, is less than 60% of the average income of all households. ....○
(c) ... whether these households are poor. .... ○
(d) ... to what extent an increase in payments would lead to increased consumption expenditures. .... ○

1.2 Data Basis of Empirical Economic Research

1.2.1. `Multiple Choice`
In order to translate real phenomena such as economic activity into concrete numbers like GDP, a series of considerations are necessary. **No** relevant step in this process is ...

(a) ... the economic theory (the concept). ○
(b) ... the selection of measurable attributes. ○
(c) ... the measurement or estimation of values. ○
(d) ... the adjustment of the obtained values (data) to the theory. ○

1.2.2. `Multiple Choice`

The requirement for data in empirical economic research to make statements about a real phenomenon in terms of a defined concept is called ...

(a) ... validity. ○
(b) ... reliability. ○
(c) ... regressivity. ○
(d) ... objectivity. ○

1.2.3. `Multiple Choice`

The requirement for a process to generate data in empirical economic research that produces comparable results when repeated is called ...

(a) ... validity. ○
(b) ... reliability. ○
(c) ... regressivity. ○
(d) ... objectivity. ○

1.2.4. `Completion`

(a) The property of the data to actually provide information for a given theoretical concept is called ________________.
(b) The property of the data to be inter-subjectively verifiable is called ________________.
(c) If observations for a variable are available for different entities (households, companies) over consecutive time periods (e.g. years), it is referred to as a ________________.

1.2.5. `True or False`

The data on the number of registered unemployed people are based on a census.

(a) True ○
(b) False ○

1.2.6. `True or False`

The data from the ZEW Financial Market Test are based on a census.

(a) True ○
(b) False ○

1.2.7. `True or False`

Data for the consumer price index are collected by observation.

(a) True ○
(b) False ○

1.2.8. `True or False`

The data from the Socio-Economic Panel (SOEP) are collected through surveys.

(a) True ... ○
(b) False ... ○

1.2.9. `Completion`

(a) The fact that data collection can change economic behavior is called ________________ of data collection.
(b) When data are retrospectively corrected over time, for example, to account for new information or changed definitions, it is referred to as ________________.

1.2.10. `Multiple Choice`

The calculation and substantive interpretation of the mean and variance is theoretically well-founded and substantively meaningful for the variable ...

(a) ... field of study. ... ○
(b) ... rating class. ... ○
(c) ... gross monthly income. ... ○
(d) ... bicycle brand. ... ○

1.2.11. `Multiple Choice`

For the quality of data collected through one's own surveys, it **does not** matter whether ...

(a) ... qualitative or quantitative characteristics are collected. ... ○
(b) ... the selected survey units are representative of the population. ... ○
(c) ... the survey units from which data is obtained are representative of the population. ... ○
(d) ... the questions are targeted, clear, neutral, and easy to answer. ... ○

1.2.12. `True or False`

For official statistics data, one can always assume that all relevant data requirements are met, regardless of the specific application.

(a) True ... ○
(b) False ... ○

1.2.13. `Multiple Choice`

When data is collected through one's own surveys (for example, postal, phone, or online surveys), the representativeness of the sample is often emphasized. In which case is the representativeness of the sample with regard to the population for certain characteristics (e.g., age and gender of the respondents) guaranteed?

(a) The respondents have the same age structure and the same proportion of women and men as the population. ... ○
(b) The age structure in the sample matches that of the population. ... ○
(c) The proportion of women and men in the sample matches the corresponding proportion of respondents. ... ○
(d) The age structure and the proportion of women and men in the sample match those of the population. ... ○

1.2.14. `True or False`

In a census through a postal questionnaire, representativeness is always guaranteed.

(a) True ○

(b) False ○

1.2.15. `Multiple Choice`

For a survey conducted on the economic consequences of the Covid-19 pandemic, in which the websites of more than 1 million German companies were analyzed, the question of the representativeness of the sample arose. When is representativeness of the sample with regard to the population of all German companies for certain characteristics (e.g. company size and sector affiliation) guaranteed?

(a) If the structure of the companies in terms of the size of the company and the affiliation of the sector, for which a web address (URL) was available, matches that of the population. ○

(b) If the structure of the companies in terms of company size and sector affiliation, whose websites could be analyzed, matches that of the population. ○

(c) If the structure of the companies in terms of company size and sector affiliation, whose websites could be analyzed, matches that of the companies for which web addresses (URLs) were available. ○

(d) Representativeness is guaranteed in this case due to the very large sample size. ○

1.2.16. `Multiple Choice`

For the preparation of political decisions to prevent deaths due to COVID-19, various data were available in December 2020:

A Quarterly data on GDP for Germany from the Federal Statistical Office

B Weekly survey data from the German Chamber of Commerce and Industry (DIHK) on the impact of business closures on companies

C Number of deaths due to or with COVID-19 in the last 7 days.

D Proportion of positive results from PCR tests conducted in the last 7 days

E Extra number from the last Lotto 6 out of 49 drawing.

Which of the following orderings of the variables seems most appropriate with regard to the quality of the variables (particularly in terms of validity and timely availability) for the specific application purpose ($A > B$ means that variable A is better suited than B)?

(a) $A > B > C > D > E$ ○

(b) $E > B > D > A > C$ ○

(c) $D > C > B > A > E$ ○

(d) $D > E > A > B > C$ ○

(e) $C > A > B > D > E$ ○

1.3 Data Processing

1.3.1. `Multiple Choice`

No method for information compression for data is ...

(a) ... the calculation of statistics such as the mean or variance. .... ◯
(b) ... the calculation of ratios. .... ◯
(c) ... storing the data in a data base. .... ◯
(d) ... a graphic presentation. .... ◯

1.3.2. `Completion`

(a) If missing values in a time series are calculated as averages of neighboring values, this is called ______________________.
(b) If a time series is extrapolated into the future using a fitted linear or nonlinear trend, this is called an ______________________.
(c) The relative change of a variable y in response to a 1% relative change in variable x is referred to as ______________________ of y with respect to x.

1.3.3. `Multiple Choice`

No advantage of using ratios is ...

(a) ... the resulting elimination of trends. .... ◯
(b) ... the resulting independence from the absolute level of the data. .... ◯
(c) ... the resulting independence from the development of the denominator. . ◯
(d) ... the resulting independence from the chosen units. .... ◯

1.3.4. `Multiple Choice`

No result of forming a ratio is ...

(a) ... the unemployment rate. .... ◯
(b) ... the gross domestic product per capita. .... ◯
(c) ... the equity ratio of a bank. .... ◯
(d) ... the number of female board members in DAX companies. .... ◯

1.3.5. `True or False`

If the growth rates are calculated in the usual way, that is

$$\Delta x_t = (x_t - x_{t-1})/x_{t-1} \times 100\,,$$

the growth rate over several periods is exactly equal to the sum of the growth rates for the individual periods.

(a) True .... ◯
(b) False .... ◯

1.3.6. `True or False`

If the price level P increases with time, measuring the inflation rate at time t using formula $(P_t - P_{t-1})/P_{t-1}$ yields higher values compared to formula $(P_t - P_{t-1})/P_t$.

(a) True .... ◯
(b) False .... ◯

1.3.7. `Completion`

(a) If a price index is calculated based on the fixed weights of a basket of goods defined for a base year, it is called a ____________ ______________________________ price index.

(b) If a price index is calculated based on the weights of the current year, it is called a ____ price index.

1.3.8. `Multiple Choice`

The shopping basket effect states that ...

(a) ... for a given budget, only a limited number of consumer goods can be purchased. .... ○

(b) ... demand for goods increases as prices rise. .... ○

(c) ... a hedonic price index overestimates price developments, as goods with falling prices are weighted too heavily. .... ○

(d) ... a Laspeyres index overestimates price developments, since the weighting of goods with falling prices tends to be too low. .... ○

1.3.9. `True or False`

If consumers buy relatively more expensive goods less frequently and relatively cheaper goods more frequently over time, this leads to the so-called "shopping basket effect" in the Laspeyres index. In the case of positive inflation rates, this leads to the inflation rate calculated using the Laspeyres index being higher than the one calculated using the Paasche index.

(a) True .... ○

(b) False .... ○

1.3.10. `True or False`

Ratios such as the unemployment rate, the export ratio, or the government debt ratio are proportions and therefore the values of these ratios always lie between 0 and 1.

(a) True .... ○

(b) False .... ○

1.4 Economic Indicators

1.4.1. `Completion`

(a) The requirement for an economic indicator to have a theoretical justification for the relationship with the phenomenon it is meant to describe is called ________________________________.

(b) A relatively stable temporal relationship historically observed between the indicator and the reference variable describes the indicator property of ________________________________.

1.4.2. `Multiple Choice`

What requirement for a business cycle indicator is **not** fulfilled by the Gross Domestic Product (GDP)?

(a) Plausibility. .... ◯
(b) Conformity. .... ◯
(c) Timely availability. .... ◯
(d) Concurrency. .... ◯

1.4.3. `Multiple Choice`

The two panels of Fig. 1.1 show standardized values of the annual growth rate of GDP (thin blue line) and an indicator from the ifo Institute surveys (red line). Which of the following statements most accurately describes the properties of the ifo Institute's variables as indicators for GDP? Pay special attention to the period around the 2008 financial crisis.

(a) The ifo Business Climate and ifo Business Expectations are always clear leading indicators. .... ◯
(b) The ifo Business Climate is a concurrent and the ifo Business Expectations are a trailing indicator. .... ◯
(c) The ifo Business Climate is a concurrent and the ifo Business Expectations are a leading indicator. .... ◯
(d) The ifo Business Climate is a leading and the ifo Business Expectations are a trailing indicator. .... ◯

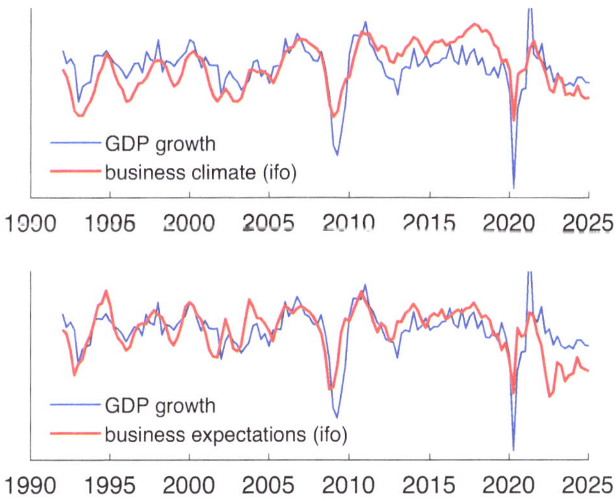

Source: Data from LSGE®Workspace; own calculations.

Fig. 1.1 Growth rates of GDP and indicators from ifo surveys. (Source: Data from LSGE®Workspace; own calculations)

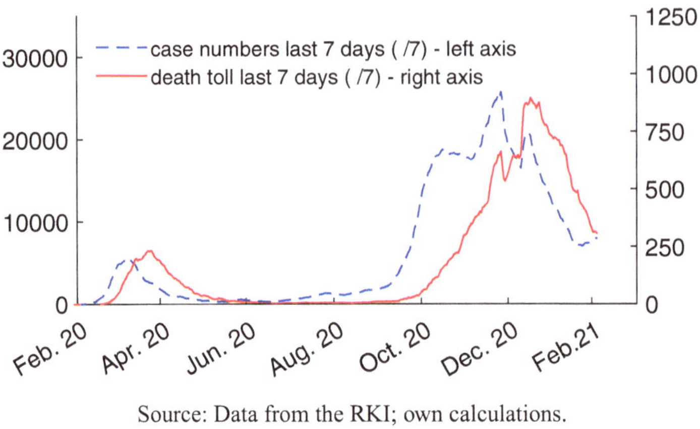

Fig. 1.2 Number of new reported cases and deaths of COVID-19. (Source: Data from the RKI; own calculations)

1.4.4. `Multiple Choice`

Figure 1.2 shows the number of new reported cases of COVID-19 (dashed blue line) and deaths (red line) over 7 days (each divided by 7).

Which of the following statements best describes the characteristics of the two indicators, case numbers and deaths?

(a) Case numbers are a leading indicator of deaths. .... ○
(b) Case numbers are a concurrent indicator for deaths. .... ○
(c) Deaths are a leading indicator for case numbers. .... ○
(d) There is no relationship between the time course of the two indicators. ... ○

1.4.5. `Multiple Choice`

No concurrent indicator for the economic cycle is ...

(a) ... the index of net production. .... ○
(b) ... the change in capacity utilization. .... ○
(c) ... the number of unemployed. .... ○
(d) ... retail sales. .... ○

1.4.6. `Multiple Choice`

A trailing indicator for the economic cycle is ...

(a) ... the number of insolvencies. .... ○
(b) ... the change in capacity utilization. .... ○
(c) ... the index of net production. .... ○
(d) ... the DAX stock index. .... ○

1.4.7. `Multiple Choice`

For macroeconomic analysis in 2020, in addition to GDP, various other indicators were used, including a weekly activity index developed by the Deutsche Bundesbank, which includes, for example, the volume of truck transport (based on toll data). Which of the following is **not** an advantage of such an indicator?

(a) The activity index is available earlier than the first GDP estimates after the end of the quarter. .... ○

(b) The activity index is a leading indicator, i.e., highs and lows occur earlier than in the GDP series. .... ○

(c) The activity index is available at a higher frequency, i.e., weekly instead of quarterly. .... ○

(d) The activity index closely follows quarterly economic developments over longer periods of time. .... ○

1.4.8. `True or False`

The public expenditure ratio is a real ratio.

(a) True .... ○

(b) False .... ○

1.4.9. `Multiple Choice`

Not a component of the balance of payments is ...

(a) ... the balance sheet of the ECB. .... ○

(b) ... the services balance. .... ○

(c) ... the capital account. .... ○

(d) ... the current account. .... ○

1.4.10. `Completion`

(a) Consumer price inflation that excludes energy and seasonal food is called ____________________.

(b) The ratio of job vacancies reported to employment agencies to all job vacancies is called ____________________.

(c) The indicator "mean duration of unemployment" is calculated by dividing the number of unemployed persons in a month by the ____________________ of the same month.

1.4.11. `Multiple Choice`

In its 2017/18 Annual Report, the German Council of Economic Experts dealt extensively with the topic of "shortage of skilled labor". On p. 385 it states: "For none of the qualification levels 'skilled workers', 'specialists' and 'experts' there are signs of a shortage between occupations and regions, since more than two unemployed individuals with appropriate qualifications are available per vacancy.' What can be inferred from this statement about the phenomenon of a "shortage of skilled labor"?

(a) The German Council of Economic Experts uses the time to fill a vacancy as a concurrent indicator of a "shortage of skilled labor". .... ○
(b) In Germany in 2018, there are clear signs of a cross-occupational and cross-regional shortage of skilled labor. .... ○
(c) The number of job vacancies is a valid indicator for the existence of a "shortage of skilled labor". .... ○
(d) The variable "shortage of skilled labor" is operationalized by the number of unemployed individuals with appropriate qualifications divided by the number of job vacancies. .... ○

1.4.12. `True or False`

In the medium term, a country's current account balance and capital account balance develop in approximately equal magnitude but with opposite signs, that is, a current account surplus is generally matched by a negative capital account balance of approximately equal size.

(a) True .... ○
(b) False .... ○

1.4.13. `Multiple Choice`

No growth indicator is ...

(a) ... the GDP. .... ○
(b) ... the production index for manufacturing. .... ○
(c) ... the capacity utilization rate. .... ○
(d) ... the public expenditure ratio. .... ○

1.4.14. `Multiple Choice`

Figure 1.3 shows different lines (A – E) in a unit square, including the diagonal as a dotted line.

Which of these lines **cannot** be the result of constructing a Lorenz curve for income data for some group of people?

(a) B and C. .... ○
(b) A and E. .... ○
(c) B and D. .... ○
(d) D and E. .... ○

1.4.15. `Multiple Choice`

The Gini coefficient ...

(a) ... is a measure of the functional income distribution. .... ○
(b) ... can take values between -1 and +1. .... ○
(c) ... decreases with increasing inequality. .... ○
(d) ... takes the value 0 when there is perfect equality. .... ○

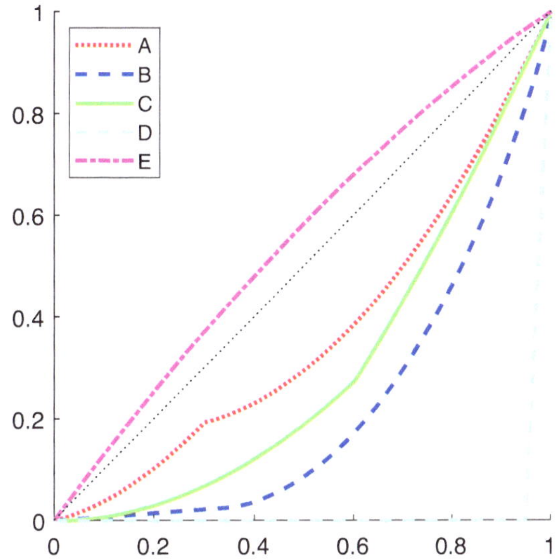

Fig. 1.3 Lorenz curves

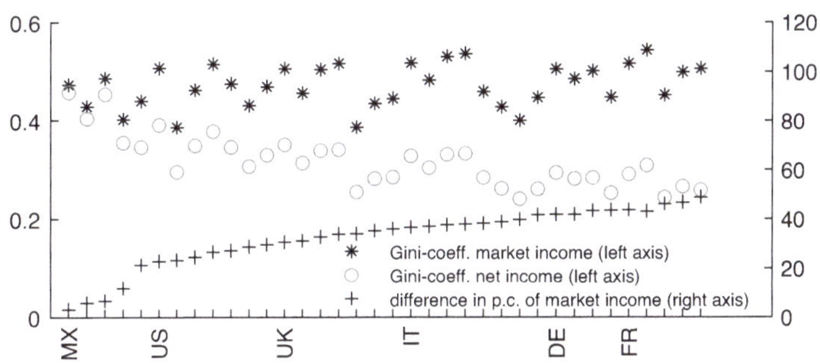

Fig. 1.4 Gini coefficients for different countries. (Source: Annual Report of the German Council of Economic Experts 2019/20, p. 321)

1.4.16. `Multiple Choice`

Figure 1.4 is based on a graph from the Annual Report 2019/20 of the German Council of Economic Experts (p. 321).

Which of the following statements regarding the countries USA (US) and Germany (DE) is therefore correct?

(a) Market incomes in Germany are approximately at the same level as in the United States, but net incomes are significantly lower in Germany. .... ○

(b) Redistribution through taxes, contributions, and transfers leads to a more significant reduction in income inequality in Germany, as measured by the Gini coefficient, than in the USA. .... ○

(c) Income inequality as measured by the Gini coefficient is significantly higher for market incomes in Germany than in the USA. .... ○
(d) Income inequality as measured by the Gini coefficient is approximately the same for net incomes in Germany and the USA. .... ○

1.4.17. `True or False`

The adjusted wage share is a measure of the distribution of personal income.
(a) True .... ○
(b) False .... ○

1.4.18. `Completion`

(a) The ratio of employee compensation to national income is called ______________________.

(b) Let x_i be the incomes of n individuals $i = 1, \ldots, n$, sorted in ascending order, that is, $x_1 \leq x_2 \leq \ldots x_n$. Let $u_j = j/n$ denote the share of the first j individuals of the total population and v_j the cumulative income share of the first j individuals of total income. The curve connecting the points $(0, 0)$, (u_1, v_1), (u_2, v_2),...,(u_n, v_n) is called the ______________________.

1.4.19. `Multiple Choice`

No measure of absolute concentration is ...
(a) ... the Herfindahl index. .... ○
(b) ... the concentration ratio CR_3. .... ○
(c) ... the Gini coefficient. .... ○
(d) ... the concentration ratio CR_5. .... ○

1.4.20. `Multiple Choice`

Figure 1.5 provides information on the European banking sector. The bars show the share of the five largest credit institutions in each country in the total assets of the banking sector for the years 2008, 2014, and 2015.
Based on the information from the figure, Which of the following statements regarding credit institutions in Belgium (*BE*) and Germany (*DE*) is correct?
(a) Concentration in the banking sector measured by the concentration ratio CR_5 increased in both countries between 2008 and 2015. .... ○
(b) The concentration in the banking sector measured by the concentration ratio CR_5 decreased in Belgium between 2008 and 2015, while it increased in Germany. .... ○
(c) The concentration in the banking sector measured by the concentration ratio CR_5 increased in Belgium between 2008 and 2015, while it decreased in Germany. .... ○
(d) A statement about the concentration in the banking sector of the two countries can only be made based on the Herfindahl index, which is not shown here. ○

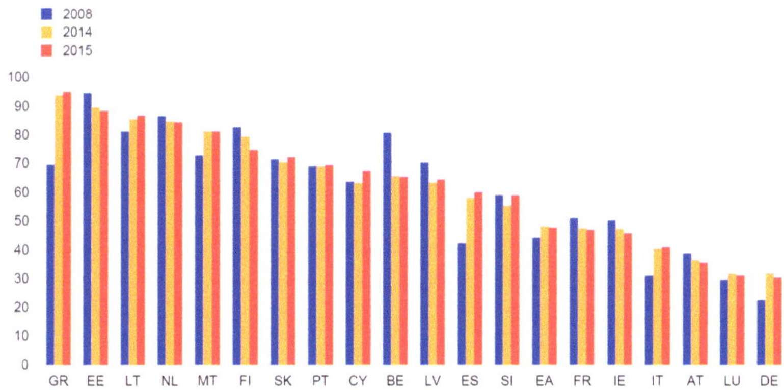

Source: ECB, Report on financial structures, October 2016, p. 30.

Fig. 1.5 Concentration in the European banking sector. (Source: ECB, Report on financial structures, October 2016, p. 30)

1.4.21. `Multiple Choice`

Which of the following statements about inequality or concentration measures is **not** correct?

(a) For a given sector, the concentration ratio CR_5 is always greater than or equal to the concentration ratio CR_3. .... ◯

(b) The concentration ratio CR_5 is a relative concentration measure. .... ◯

(c) For the Gini coefficient, higher values indicate a higher level of inequality. .... ◯

(d) The Gini coefficient can be calculated based on the Lorenz curve. .... ◯

1.4.22. `True or False`

The insolvency rate and the capacity utilization rate are both trailing indicators of overall economic activity.

(a) True .... ◯

(b) False .... ◯

1.5 Input-Output Analysis

1.5.1. `Multiple Choice`

No common extension of input-output analysis is ...

(a) ... the analysis of international input-output tables. .... ◯

(b) ... the dynamic analysis in which input factors change over time, e.g., due to investments in capital stock. .... ◯

(c) ... the endogenous modeling of factor demand. .... ◯

(d) ... the adjustment of input coefficients to theoretical target values. .... ◯

1.5.2. `Completion`

(a) The number that measures the share of production of sector i going as input into sector j or to the final use component j is called ______________________.

(b) The number that indicates the share of inputs from sector i in the cost structure of sector j is called ______________.

1.5.3. `True or False`

The Leontief inverse can be used to determine the changes in the production values of all sectors induced by changes in final demand.

(a) True .... ○
(b) False .... ○

1.5.4. `Multiple Choice`

Input-output analysis can be used to answer the question ...

(a) ... how much value added in the textile industry is induced by furniture production. .... ○
(b) ... what the profit-maximizing combination of production factors looks like. .... ○
(c) ... whether an increase in VAT leads to a reduction in public debt. .... ○
(d) ... whether factor incomes (wages, profits) are fairly distributed among input factors. .... ○

1.5.5. `Multiple Choice`

A current input-output table does **not** provide information on ...

(a) ... the input factors used for the production of goods. .... ○
(b) ... the development of capital productivity in individual sectors. .... ○
(c) ... the Input-Output linkages between sectors. .... ○
(d) ... the final use of the goods and services produced. .... ○

1.5.6. `Multiple Choice`

Not a concept in the context of input-output analysis is ...

(a) ... the output coefficient. .... ○
(b) ... the Leontief inverse. .... ○
(c) ... the Kronecker product. .... ○
(d) ... the Input-Ouput linkages between sectors. .... ○

1.5.7. `True or False`

Input-output analysis can be used to quantify the transmission effects of production declines in the service sector caused by business closures in sectors of the manufacturing industry during the COVID-19 pandemic.

(a) True .... ○
(b) False .... ○

1.6 The Econometric Model

1.6.1. `Multiple Choice`

Which of the following components is **not** part of every econometric analysis?

(a) an economic model. ○
(b) suitable data. ○
(c) seasonal adjustment. ○
(d) statistical theories and methods. ○

1.6.2. `Multiple Choice`

No step in the process of setting up, quantifying, and evaluating an econometric model is ...

(a) ... the estimation of parameters. ○
(b) ... the maximization of the sum of squared residuals. ○
(c) ... the specification of the model. ○
(d) ... the review of the estimation based on the estimated residuals. ○

1.6.3. `Multiple Choice`

Which statement about the econometric model is **not** true?

(a) The expected value of the error terms should be zero. ○
(b) The econometric model should be derived from theoretical considerations. ○
(c) The error terms should reflect random, unsystematic influences on the explanatory variables. ○
(d) The parameters to be estimated are chosen in the least squares estimation so that the sum of squared residuals is maximized. ○

1.6.4. `True or False`

An econometric model does not require a theoretical understanding of a potential relationship between the modeled variables.

(a) True ○
(b) False ○

1.6.5. `Multiple Choice`

Which statement about the error terms of an econometric model is **not** true?

(a) The error terms reflect the influence of all factors which are not considered explicitly in the model. ○
(b) Error terms can take on positive and negative values. ○
(c) The expected value of the error terms is zero. ○
(d) The sum of all realized error terms (residuals) is positive expect in the case of a perfect fit of the model to the data, when it is zero. ○

1.6.6. `Multiple Choice`

Which type of presentation is **not** suited to represent the quality of the fit in a linear regression model for time series with a single explanatory variable?

(a) Histogram of the dependent variable. ○

(b) Histogram of the residuals. ○
(c) Scatterplot of explanatory and dependent variable. ○
(d) Time series plot of dependent variable (y) and model fit ($\hat{y}$). ○

1.6.7. `Multiple Choice`
Consider the linear regression model

$$Y_t = \beta_1 + \beta_2 X_t + \varepsilon_t \, .$$

Which of the following statements regarding an estimate $\hat{\beta}_2$ is correct?
(a) $\hat{\beta}_2$ corresponds to the most likely value of β_2. ○
(b) If X_t increases by 1 unit, the expected value of Y_t changes by $\hat{\beta}_2$ units if all else remains unchanged (ceteris paribus). ○
(c) If $\hat{\beta}_2 = 0$, this proofs that X_t has no relevant impact on Y_t. ○
(d) If $\hat{\beta}_2 \neq 0$, this proofs that X_t has a relevant impact on Y_t. ○

1.7 The Linear Regression Model

1.7.1. `True or False`
If the linear model $Y_t = \beta + \varepsilon_t$ is estimated for a time series Y_t using the least squares method, then the estimator $\hat{\beta}$ for the coefficient β is **not** equal to the arithmetic mean of the observations of Y_t.
(a) True ○
(b) False ○

1.7.2. `Completion`
(a) An estimator that produces the true value of the parameter in the population on average over many samples is an ______________________ estimator.
(b) An estimator is called ______________________ if it achieves the lowest variance within a given group of estimators.

1.7.3. `Multiple Choice`
If the value of the coefficient of determination R^2 is less than 0.5 (50%), then ...
(a) ... this indicates the presence of pronounced heteroskedasticity. ○
(b) ... at least one additional explanatory variable must be added to the model for the OLS estimator to have the `BLUE` property. ○
(c) ... endogeneity is likely present. ○
(d) ... none of the above statements is correct. ○

1.7.4. `True or False`
The R^2 cannot decrease when additional variables are added.
(a) True ○
(b) False ○

1.7.5. **Multiple Choice**

The value of the coefficient of determination R^2 for the linear regression model $Y_t = \beta_1 + \beta_2 X_t + \varepsilon_t$ will be approximately zero if ...

(a) ... the values of Y_t and X_t are small. .... ◯
(b) ... the value of β_1 is close to zero. .... ◯
(c) ... the values of ε_t are small. .... ◯
(d) ... the value of β_2 is close to zero. .... ◯

1.7.6. **Multiple Choice**

Consider a model that assumes a linear relationship between Y_t and X_t, i.e., $Y_t = \beta_1 + \beta_2 X_t$. Observations for Y_t and X_t are available for $t = 1, \ldots, T$. Which of the following statements is correct?

(a) Parameters β_1 and β_2 can be meaningfully estimated even if the observations do not lie exactly on a straight line. .... ◯
(b) If the observations do not lie exactly on a straight line, the model must be rejected because it is flawed. .... ◯
(c) If the number of observations T is (significantly) greater than 30, it can be assumed that $\beta_1 = 1$. .... ◯
(d) X_t and Y_t are correlated. No statement about a causal relationship between X_t and Y_t can be made. .... ◯

1.7.7. **True or False**

If there is a strong linear relationship between the variables X_t and Y_t, the value of the coefficient of determination R^2 must be close to + 1.

(a) True .... ◯
(b) False .... ◯

1.7.8. **Multiple Choice**

Which of the following statements about error terms and the least squares estimator is **not** correct?

(a) If $\hat{\beta}$ denotes the least squares estimator of a linear regression model, then the values $\hat{y} = x'\hat{\beta}$ are the predicted values for the dependent variable. ... ◯
(b) The error term of the model affects the observed dependent variable but cannot itself be observed. .... ◯
(c) If the least squares estimator $\hat{\beta}$ is both consistent and unbiased, then the true unknown parameter β equals $\hat{\beta}$. .... ◯
(d) From the consistency of a least squares estimator it follows that the variance of the estimator $\hat{\beta}$ decreases with increasing sample size. .... ◯

1.7.9. **True or False**

A statistically significant regression coefficient always indicates a causal influence of the associated variable on the dependent variable.

(a) True .... ◯
(b) False .... ◯

1.7.10. `Multiple Choice`

For the decomposition of the variation of a variable Y_t using a linear regression model, it holds that ...

(a) ... $TSS = RSS^2$. ○
(b) ... $TSS - RSS = ESS$. ○
(c) ... $TSS + RSS = ESS$. ○
(d) ... $TSS + ESS = -RSS$. ○

1.7.11. `Multiple Choice`

Which of the following conditions does **not** have to be fulfilled in order to interpret the coefficients estimated by the least squares method using the standard approach?

(a) The error terms are normally distributed. ○
(b) All estimated parameters are significantly different from zero. ○
(c) The error terms for different observations are independent. ○
(d) The variance of the error terms is independent of the observation. ○

1.7.12. `True or False`

In a correctly specified consumption function (with more than 50 observations), the estimated value for the marginal propensity to consume is 0.978. A standard deviation of 0.0075 is calculated for this estimated coefficient. It follows that the null hypothesis, that the marginal propensity to consume is in fact equal to one, **cannot** be rejected at the 5% significance level.

(a) True ○
(b) False ○

1.7.13. `True or False`

In a correctly specified wage function with the logarithm of hourly wages as the dependent variable (with more than 1000 observations), the estimated effect of an additional year of education is 0.07 (7%). The standard deviation of this estimated coefficient is 0.025. It follows that the null hypothesis, that the effect of an additional year of education is in fact 0.10 (10%), **cannot** be rejected at the 5% significance level.

(a) True ○
(b) False ○

1.7.14. `Multiple Choice`

Consider the linear regression model $Y_t = \beta_1 + \beta_2 X_t + \varepsilon_t$ with observations for $t = 1, \ldots, T$. The ε_t are independently and identically distributed, and the X_t are exogenous, i.e., in particular, there is no correlation between X_t and ε_t. Which of the following statements is correct for the least squares estimation?

(a) If the ε_t do not follow a normal distribution, then the least squares estimators $\hat{\beta}_1$ and $\hat{\beta}_2$ are biased. This also holds asymptotically, i.e., for $T \to \infty$. ○

(b) If the ε_t do not follow a normal distribution, then the least squares estimators $\hat{\beta}_1$ and $\hat{\beta}_2$ are biased in finite samples, e.g., for $T = 100$. Asymptotically, i.e., for $T \to \infty$, the estimators are unbiased. .... ○
(c) If the ε_t do not follow a normal distribution, the distribution of the estimator $\hat{\beta}_2$ is also not normal in finite samples. .... ○
(d) For the proof that the least squares estimator is efficient, the assumption of unbiasedness is not needed. .... ○

1.7.15. `Multiple Choice`
You want to investigate whether the money supply M3 in Switzerland is growing at the same rate as prices. To do so, you regress the logarithm of the money supply (`LOG(M)`) on the logarithm of the price level (`LOG(P)`), measured by the GDP deflator. You obtain the following results:

```
Dependent Variable: LOG(M)        Method: Least Squares
Sample: 1985:1 2020:4         Included observations: 144
-----------------------------------------------------
Variable  Coefficient  Std. Error  t-Statistic  Prob.
-----------------------------------------------------
C            -2.165750    0.739631    -2.928151   0.0040
LOG(P)        3.405758    0.163546     20.82442   0.0000
-----------------------------------------------------
```

Which of the following statements correctly describes the relationship between M and P? As usual, assume a significance level of 5% and that all assumptions for applying the ordinary least squares regression are met.
(a) The price elasticity of the money supply is **not** significantly different from 3.5. .... ○
(b) The price elasticity of the money supply is **not** significantly different from zero. .... ○
(c) A statement about the statistical significance of the coefficient of `P` is **not** possible based on the information provided. .... ○
(d) The model constant (`C`) is not significantly different from zero. .... ○

1.7.16. `Multiple Choice`
In order to test the null hypothesis in a linear regression model that a group of variables has no joint effect on the dependent variable (i.e., that the coefficients associated with these variables are all equal to zero), one uses:
(a) the probit method. .... ○
(b) the logit method. .... ○
(c) the F-test. .... ○
(d) the Jarque-Bera test. .... ○

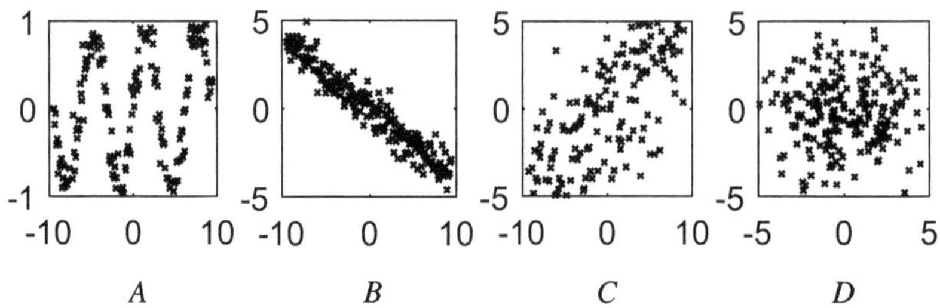

Fig. 1.6 Bivariate scatterplots

1.7.17. `Completion`

(a) The ____________________________ of an estimated linear regression expresses the proportion of the explained variation in the total variation of the dependent variable.

(b) When testing several linear restrictions on parameters simultaneously in a linear regression model (e.g., joint significance), one can use the ___________ test.

1.7.18. `Multiple Choice`

Figure 1.6 shows four scatterplots of bivariate datasets. To each of these datasets, a linear regression model was fitted and the corresponding R^2 calculated. Which of the following orderings best corresponds to the models in terms of their R^2 values ($A > B$ means that R^2 for dataset A is greater than for dataset B).

(a) $B > C > A > D$. .... ○
(b) $C > B > A > D$. .... ○
(c) $B > A > C > D$. .... ○
(d) $A > D > B > C$. .... ○

1.8 Residual Analysis and Check of Model Assumptions

1.8.1. `Multiple Choice`

If you want to test whether the residuals of a regression model could be realizations of normally distributed error terms, you use ...

(a) ... dummy variables for different distributional assumptions. .... ○
(b) ... the Durbin-Watson test. .... ○
(c) ... the Jarque-Bera test. .... ○
(d) ... the method of variance stabilization by logarithmizing. .... ○

1.8.2. `True or False`

If a graphical analysis of the residuals shows that the residuals tend to lie above or below the zero line for several consecutive periods, this is an indication of autocorrelation in the residuals.

(a) True .... ○
(b) False .... ○

1.8.3. `True or False`

If a time series of error terms ε_t does not exhibit first-order autocorrelation, the error terms are independent.

(a) True .... ○
(b) False .... ○

1.8.4. `True or False`

If a graphical analysis of the residuals of a regression with time series shows that the absolute magnitude of the residuals tends to increase over time, this is an indication of autocorrelation in the residuals.

(a) True .... ○
(b) False .... ○

1.8.5. `Completion`

(a) The standard test reported for the first-order autocorrelation of residuals in a linear regression model is called the ______________________

____________.

(b) A common test for heteroskedasticity in the residuals of a linear regression model, in which the squared residuals are regressed on the explanatory variables of the model, their squares and interaction terms, is called the ______________________ test.

(c) If a dynamic model is to be tested for autocorrelation of the residuals, the ____________________________ test can be used.

1.8.6. `Multiple Choice`

Estimating a simple consumption function using seasonally adjusted data for private consumption (`CONS_SA`) and disposable income (`Y_DISP_SA`) for the period 2010.1 to 2020.4 leads to the following results:

```
Dependent Variable: CONS_SA        Method: Least Squares
Sample: 2010:1 2020:4          Included observations:  44
-------------------------------------------------------
Variable    Coefficient   Std. Error   t-Statistic   Prob.
-------------------------------------------------------
C             61.04208     15.80613      3.861924   0.0004
Y_DISP_SA     0.756471     0.034879      21.68853   0.0000
       -------------------------------------------------------
R-squared              0.9180   Mean dependent var    402.58
Adjusted R-squared 0.9161   S.D. dependent var    31.160
Log likelihood       -158.22   Durbin-Watson stat    0.8013
F-statistic            470.39   Prob(F-statistic)     0.0000
-------------------------------------------------------
```

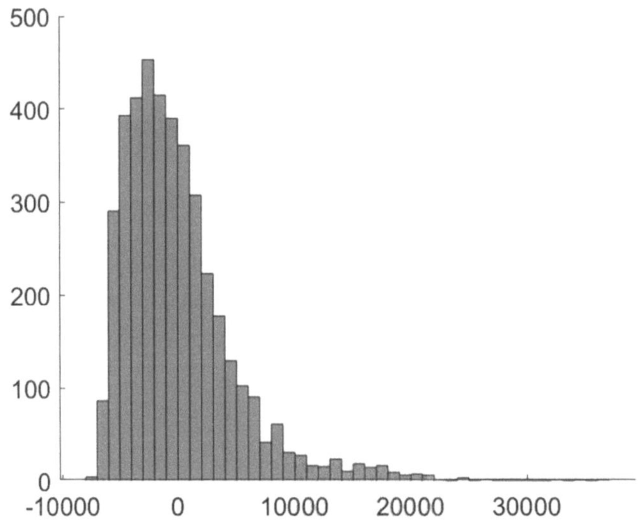

Fig. 1.7 Histogram of residuals of rent equation. (Source: Data from GSOEP; own calculations)

Which of the following statements about the consumption function is **not** correct based on the information provided?

(a) The marginal propensity to consume is significantly less than one. .... ○
(b) The model's error terms exhibit first-order autocorrelation. .... ○
(c) All explanatory variables in the model jointly have a statistically significant influence on consumption. .... ○
(d) Due to the very high R^2, the presence of heteroskedasticity can be ruled out. ○

1.8.7. `Multiple Choice`

After estimating a linear regression model to explain rent payments by a constant and gross wage income of 4139 individuals in Germany, the residuals are analyzed. Figure 1.7 shows the histogram of the residuals. In addition, the econometric software provides further information about the residuals:

$$\text{Skewness} = 1.7560, \qquad \text{Kurtosis} = 7.975$$
$$\text{Jarque-Bera} = 6396.02, \text{ Probability} = 0.0000$$

Which of the following statements is **not** correct based on the information provided?

(a) The histogram indicates a right skewed distribution. .... ○
(b) The null hypothesis "H_0: Error terms are homoscedastic" has to be rejected at the 5% level. .... ○
(c) The null hypothesis "H_0: Error terms follow a normal distribution" has to be rejected at the 5% level. .... ○
(d) A statement about possible autocorrelation of error terms is not feasible based on the available information. .... ○

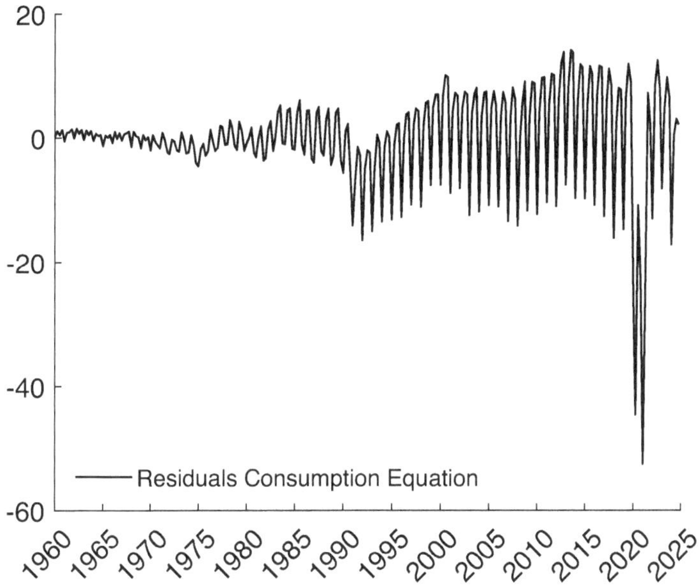

Source: Data from Destatis; own calculations.

Fig. 1.8 Residuals of consumption equation. (Source: Data from Destatis; own calculations)

1.8.8. `Multiple Choice`

Figure 1.8 shows a time series plot of the residuals of a linear regression model with consumption as dependent and disposable income as explanatory variable for Germany (1960–1990 only West Germany).

Which of the following statements is **not** correct based on the information provided?

(a) The development of the residuals over time indicates an increase in residuals variance, i.e. heteroskedasticity. .... ○
(b) The residuals exhibit a seasonal pattern. .... ○
(c) The development of the residuals over time suggests autocorrelation of order 4. .... ○
(d) The figure allows the conclusion that the null hypothesis of a normal distribution of the error terms does not has to be rejected at the 5% level. .... ○

1.9 Qualitative Variable

1.9.1. `Multiple Choice`

What is meant by a dummy variable?

(a) A variable that has exactly two discrete outcomes (e.g. smoker or non-smoker). .... ○

(b) A variable that has more than two discrete outcomes (e.g. blood type A, B, AB, or 0). .... ○
(c) A variable without substantive meaning that is assigned to the constant in a regression model. .... ○
(d) The error term, which as a "dumb variable" captures all effects not included in the model. .... ○

1.9.2. `Multiple Choice`

A linear regression analysis is used to examine the factors that influence the number of sick days per year for employed persons. The proposed model is as follows:

$$\text{SD}_i = \beta_0 + \beta_1\text{DMAN}_i + \beta_2\text{DWOMAN}_i + \beta_3\text{AGE}_i + \beta_4\text{GIESSEN}_i + \varepsilon_i \,.$$

Here, SD_i denotes the number of sick days per year for person i, DMAN_i is a dummy variable that takes the value one for men and zero for women, DWOMAN_i is a dummy that takes the value one for women and zero for men, AGE_i is the age in years, and GIESSEN_i is a dummy that equals one if a Giessen university degree is present and zero otherwise.
What problem is to be expected in this model specification?

(a) Positive autocorrelation of error terms. .... ○
(b) Negative autocorrelation of the error terms. .... ○
(c) Perfect multicollinearity. .... ○
(d) The estimator for coefficient β_4 is not between zero and one. .... ○

1.9.3. `True or False`

In estimating the linear probability model, it may happen that the model predicts probabilities for the outcome value one of a binary dependent variable that exceed 100%.

(a) True .... ○
(b) False .... ○

1.9.4. `Multiple Choice`

Let i be a person index, ε_i an error term, and D_i^{woman} a dummy variable that takes the value 1 if the person i is a woman. The following wage regression is estimated: $\text{wage}_i = \beta_0 + \beta_1 D_i^{woman} + \varepsilon_i$. For the resulting estimators $\hat{\beta}_0$ and $\hat{\beta}_1$, the following holds:

(a) $\hat{\beta}_0$ is the expected wage for men, and $\hat{\beta}_1$ is the expected wage for women. .... ○
(b) $\hat{\beta}_0 - \hat{\beta}_1$ is the expected wage for men, and $\hat{\beta}_1$ is the expected wage for women. .... ○
(c) $\hat{\beta}_0$ is the expected wage for men, and $\hat{\beta}_1 - \hat{\beta}_0$ is the expected wage for women. .... ○
(d) $\hat{\beta}_0$ is the expected wage for men, and $\hat{\beta}_0 + \hat{\beta}_1$ is the expected wage for women. .... ○

1.9.5. `Multiple Choice`

What assumption regarding the distribution function of the error terms in the latent variable model underlies the Probit model?

(a) The Pareto distribution. .... ○
(b) The uniform distribution. .... ○
(c) The normal distribution. .... ○
(d) The logistic distribution. .... ○

1.9.6. `True or False`

The coefficients estimated in the linear probability model indicate by what value the probability of a dependent variable changes when the explanatory variable belonging to the coefficient increases by one.

(a) True .... ○
(b) False .... ○

1.9.7. `Multiple Choice`

An empirical study aims to determine how different leadership styles affect company profits. Data were collected for 120 small and medium-sized companies, each containing the 2019 profit P_i and an indicator L_i for a firm i, which can take values 1, 2 or 3, where 1 represents an authoritarian, 2 a cooperative and 3 a laissez-faire leadership style. Sales revenue R_i in 2019 was also collected as an explanatory variable.

In the estimation of the model

$$\log(P_i) = \beta_1 + \beta_2 \log(R_i) + \beta_3 L_i + \varepsilon_i$$

the following parameter estimates were obtained:

$$\beta_1 = -0.1, \beta_2 = 1.1 \text{ and } \beta_3 = 0.2\,.$$

The standard deviation of all estimators is less than 0.02, so assuming that all assumptions for using the ordinary least squares method hold (which you may assume), all three coefficients are statistically significantly different from zero. Which of the following statements is thus correct based on the available information?

(a) The revenue elasticity of profit is significantly less than 1. .... ○
(b) A cooperative leadership style is preferable to both the authoritarian and the laissez-faire styles, as it leads to higher profits ceteris paribus (i.e. at equal revenue). .... ○
(c) The model assumes that the change in profit at given revenue (i.e. ceteris paribus) is exactly the same in the following two cases: switching from an authoritarian to a cooperative leadership style and switching from a cooperative to a laissez-faire style. .... ○

(d) The interpretation of the estimates would not change if the coding of leadership styles were changed as follows: 1—authoritarian, 2—laissez-faire and 3—cooperative. ○

1.9.8. `Multiple Choice`

Which method is typically used for estimating the Probit and Logit models?

(a) The ordinary least squares method (OLS). ○
(b) The estimator based on minimizing absolute deviations (LAD). ○
(c) The method of moments (MM). ○
(d) The maximum likelihood method (ML). ○

1.9.9. `Multiple Choice`

The effect of a variable X_i on the binary dependent variable D_i is to be investigated. The linear probability model $D_i = \beta_0 + \beta_1 X_i + \varepsilon_i$ is estimated. Furthermore, the relationship is also estimated using a logit model, which reports the estimated coefficient $\hat{\alpha}_1$ for X_i. For $\hat{\alpha}_1$ and $\hat{\beta}_1$, we have ...

(a) ... $\hat{\beta}_1$ and $\hat{\alpha}_1$ each measure the marginal effect of increasing X_i by one unit on the probability that $D_i = 1$. ○
(b) ... if $\hat{\alpha}_1 < 0$, then the probability that $D_i = 1$ decreases with increasing values of X_i. ○
(c) ... $\hat{\alpha}_1 = \hat{\beta}_1$. ○
(d) ... $\hat{\alpha}_1 + \hat{\beta}_1 = 1$. ○

1.9.10. `Multiple Choice`

Figure 1.9 shows an excerpt from the estimation results of a Probit model presented by N. Barasinska and D. Schäfer in Discussion Paper No 05/2013 of the Deutsche Bundesbank. The dependent variable `RISKY` takes the value zero if the person under consideration does not hold risky investments (e.g. equity funds), and the value one if he or she does.

The results reported in Fig. 1.9 are based on data from individuals in Austria. `Male` denotes a dummy variable equal to one for men and zero otherwise, `ln(Income)` refers to the logarithm of a person's income, the dummies `II Wealth quartile`, `III Wealth quartile`, and `IV Wealth quartile` indicate membership in the respective quartile of the wealth distribution, the dummy `Real Property` indicates real estate ownership, the dummy `Self-Employed` refers to self-employment, and the dummy `Education` captures a higher educational qualification. The equation includes additional explanatory variables not shown here.

The reported values are the marginal effects of the respective variable evaluated at the country-specific mean of all explanatory variables. The symbols *, **, and *** denote statistical significance at the levels 10%, 5%, and 1%, respectively.

Which of the following statements is correct on the basis of the available information?

Fig. 1.9 Results of Probit model. (Source: Barasinska and Schäfer (2013))

Male	0.039***
	(0.014)
ln(Income)	0.095***
	(0.018)
II Wealth quartile	0.129***
	(0.037)
III Wealth quartile	0.258***
	(0.04)
IV Wealth quartile	0.524***
	(0.042)
Real Property	0.042***
	(0.013)
Self-Employed	-0.001
	(0.024)
Education	0.049***
	(0.014)

Source: Barasinska and Schäfer (2013).

(a) The parameter estimator for `Male` in the Probit equation, which is not reported here, must be negative. .... ○
(b) Ceteris paribus, men have a higher probability of investing in risky asset classes. .... ○
(c) No conclusion can be drawn about the effect direction of real estate ownership. .... ○
(d) A 1% increase in income leads, ceteris paribus, to a 9.5% higher probability of investing in risky asset classes. .... ○

1.9.11. **Multiple Choice**

As part of an analysis of the determinants of wage levels, the following linear model is estimated:

$$W_i = \beta_1 + \beta_2 DSEX_i + \beta_3 DABI_i + \beta_4 DSEX_i \times DABI_i + \varepsilon_i$$

Here, W_i denotes the gross monthly wage of person i, $DSEX_i$ is a dummy variable equal to one for women and zero for men, and $DABI_i$ is a dummy variable equal to one if person i has completed the Abitur (German university entrance qualification) as their highest level of education (otherwise zero). Assume that the estimation of the model produces a significantly positive estimator $\hat{\beta}_4$. How can this be interpreted?

(a) The coefficient indicates by how much the expected wage for women with an Abitur is higher than that of women without an Abitur. .... ○
(b) The coefficient indicates by how much the expected wage of women without an Abitur is lower than that of men without an Abitur. .... ○

(c) The coefficient indicates by how much the effect of the Abitur on wages is higher for women than for men. .... ○
(d) The coefficient represents the marginal effect of an additional educational qualification that can only be obtained by women. .... ○

1.10 Trend and Seasonal Adjustment

1.10.1. `Multiple Choice`

Figure 1.10 shows the daily number of COVID-19 cases reported to the Robert Koch Institute (RKI).

Which of the following statements is correct regarding the time series of case numbers?

(a) The time series does not show any seasonal pattern. .... ○
(b) The time series shows a seasonal pattern with monthly frequency. .... ○
(c) The time series shows an additive weekly seasonal pattern. .... ○
(d) The time series shows a multiplicative (proportional) weekly seasonal pattern. .... ○

1.10.2. `True or False`

The method of "moving averages" means that each time series value x_t is "replaced" by the average of the elements in an interval surrounding x_t. This procedure "smooths out peaks".

(a) True .... ○
(b) False .... ○

1.10.3. `Multiple Choice`

Which of the following methods is **not** suitable for adjusting a time series Y_t with monthly data for its seasonal component (e.g., for graphical analysis)?

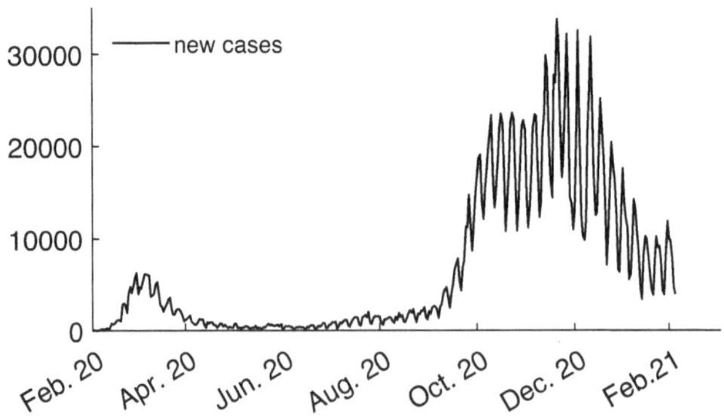

Fig. 1.10 Daily number of reported COVID-19 cases. (Source: Data from the RKI; own illustration)

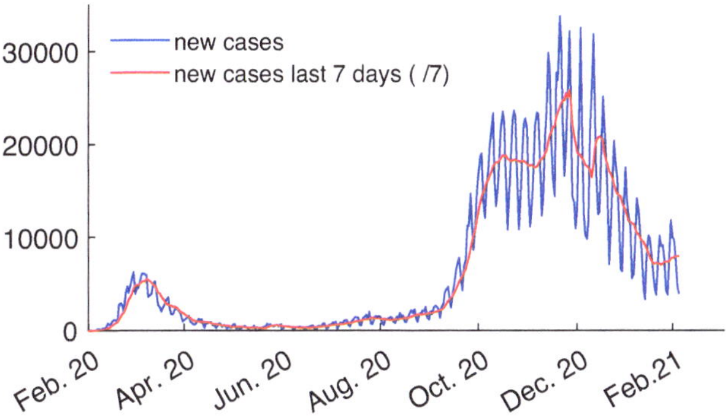

Source: Data from the RKI; own illustration.

Fig. 1.11 COVID-19 case numbers. (Source: Data from the RKI; own illustration)

(a) Calculating annual growth rates. .... ○
(b) Moving average $MA_t = (0.5Y_{t-2} + Y_{t-1} + Y_t + Y_{t+1} + 0.5Y_{t+2})/4$. .... ○
(c) Leser filter (also known as the Hodrick-Prescott filter) with smoothing parameter $\lambda = 14{,}400$. .... ○
(d) Calculating the residuals from a regression of the series on twelve monthly dummies. .... ○

1.10.4. `Multiple Choice`

Figure 1.11 shows, in addition to the daily number of cases of COVID-19 reported to the RKI (blue line), the 7-day case counts (divided by 7) reported by the RKI (red line).

Which statement about the displayed time series is **not** correct?

(a) The time series `New cases` shows a weekday effect, which is not visible in the series `7-day cases`. .... ○
(b) The calculation of `7-day cases` involves applying a moving average to the `New cases`. .... ○
(c) The black line was calculated using the Leser filter (also known as the HP filter). .... ○
(d) The black line does not result from calculating weekly growth rates. ..... ○

1.10.5. `Completion`

(a) The phenomenon where the values of the HP trend component at the current edge often change significantly when new observations are added and the HP trend component is recalculated is called ____________________.
(b) The method used for seasonal adjustment that is based on the decomposition of the time series in the frequency domain is called the ____________________ procedure.

1.10.6. `Multiple Choice`

Let y_t and x_t for $t = 1, \ldots, T$ be monthly observations of variables that include a seasonal component. Which of the following econometric models can be estimated for these data without the risk of biased t-statistics?

(a) $y_t^{mov.avg} = \beta_0 + \beta_1 x_t^{mov.avg} + \varepsilon_t$, where $y_t^{mov.avg}$ and $x_t^{mov.avg}$ are moving averages. ○

(b) $\Delta^{12} y_t = \beta_0 + \beta_1 \Delta^{12} x_t + \varepsilon_t$ for $t = 13, 14, 15, \ldots, T$, where Δ^{12} denotes changes compared to the previous year (i.e., $\Delta^{12} y_t = y_t - y_{t-12}$). ○

(c) $\Delta^{12} y_t = \beta_0 + \beta_1 \Delta^{12} x_t + \varepsilon_t$ for $t = 13, 25, 37, \ldots, T$, where Δ^{12} denotes changes compared to the previous year (i.e., $\Delta^{12} y_t = y_t - y_{t-12}$). ○

(d) $y_t^{HP} = \beta_0 + \beta_1 x_t^{HP} + \varepsilon_t$, where y_t^{HP} and x_t^{HP} denote the smoothed components of y_t and x_t obtained using the Leser filter (also known as the Hodrick-Prescott filter). ○

1.10.7. `Multiple Choice`

The use of seasonally adjusted data in time series regressions can have undesirable side effects. Consider the situation where the variables y_t and x_t are quarterly observations, not seasonally adjusted. y_t^{HP} and x_t^{HP} denote the smoothed components obtained with the HP filter, $\Delta y_t = y_t - y_{t-1}$ and $\Delta x_t = x_t - x_{t-1}$ denote quarterly changes, and $\Delta^4 y_t = y_t - y_{t-4}$ and $\Delta^4 x_t = x_t - x_{t-4}$ the changes compared to the same quarter of the previous year. Which of the following regression models can be estimated without the risk of biased test statistics?

(a) $y_t^{HP} = \beta_0 + \beta_1 x_t^{HP} + \varepsilon_t, t = 1, \ldots, T$. ○

(b) $y_t^{HP} = \beta_0 + \beta_1 x_t^{HP} + \varepsilon_t, t = 1, 5, 9, \ldots, T$. ○

(c) $\Delta^4 y_t = \beta_0 + \beta_1 \Delta^4 x_t + \varepsilon_t, t = 1, \ldots, T$. ○

(d) $\Delta^4 y_t = \beta_0 + \beta_1 \Delta^4 x_t + \varepsilon_t, t = 1, 5, 9, \ldots, T$. ○

1.10.8. `Multiple Choice`

Why should trend components estimated using some seasonal adjustment methods not be used for forecasting?

(a) The trend component on the current edge is sensitive to the inclusion of additional data points. ○

(b) The "true" value of the smoothing parameter λ is unknown. ○

(c) The trend component tends towards one for a high number of observations. ○

(d) The irregular component is mistakenly not included in the forecast. ○

1.11 Dynamic Models

1.11.1. `Multiple Choice`

The error correction model is characterized by the fact that ...

(a) ... erroneous measurements of the variables are automatically corrected. ○

(b) ... it is taken into account that econometric estimates always contain errors. .... ○

(c) ... both short-term dynamics and long-term relationships can be modeled simultaneously. .... ○

(d) ... the estimated errors (residuals) are corrected by a filtering coefficient to enable particularly robust forecasts. .... ○

1.11.2. `Multiple Choice`

You estimate an error correction model to determine the long-term effect of the oil price per barrel (`OIL`) on the gasoline price per gallon (`GASOLINE`) in the form:

$$\Delta(\texttt{GASOLINE})_t = \beta_0 + \beta_1 \Delta(\texttt{OIL})_t + \beta_2 \texttt{GASOLINE}_{t-1} + \beta_3 \texttt{OEL}_{t-1} + \varepsilon_t.$$

Here, t denotes the time index, Δ the first differences, and ε_t the error term. The estimated coefficients are: $\hat{\beta}_0 = 0.2$, $\hat{\beta}_1 = 0.02$, $\hat{\beta}_2 = -0.25$ and $\hat{\beta}_3 = 0.007$. Therefore, the long-term effect of the oil price on the gasoline price is estimated to be equal to ...

(a) 0.00175 .... ○

(b) 0.007 .... ○

(c) 0.028 .... ○

(d) 0.08 .... ○

1.11.3. `Completion`

(a) When choosing among different lag lengths K in a distributed lag model, this selection can be made based on an ___________ ______________________ criterion.

(b) The following table shows the AIC criterion values to estimate a function in which a consumer price index is modeled by seasonal dummies, as well as current and up to k lagged values of a wage index.

Lags k	1	2	3	4	5	6	7	8	9	10
AIC	3.815	3.787	3.675	3.429	3.361	3.324	3.373	3.421	3.422	3.393

Accordingly, ______________________ lagged values should be included in the estimation.

(c) The dynamic model that captures both short-term adjustment to changes in the explanatory variable(s) and a long-term stable relationship between the variables (and adjustment to it), is called ______________________.

1.11.4. `Multiple Choice`

The following table shows the result of the estimation of a consumption function, where `CONSUMPTION` stands for private consumption and `Y_DISP` for disposable income of private households in Germany.

```
Dependent Variable: CONSUMPTION  Method: Least Squares
Sample: 1991:2 2019:2        Included observations: 113
------------------------------------------------------
Variable  Coefficient  Std. Error  t-Statistic  Prob.
------------------------------------------------------
C              0.062981     1.690349     0.037259  0.9703
@SEAS(1)     -21.43596      1.113921   -19.24370   0.0000
@SEAS(2)      -8.193195     1.271604    -6.443195  0.0000
@SEAS(3)      -1.625009     0.930340    -1.746683  0.0836
Y_DISP         0.638733     0.061411    10.40097   0.0000
Y_DISP(-1)   0.278587     0.061710     4.514424  0.0000
------------------------------------------------------
R-squared              0.9980  Mean dependent var  328.46
Adjusted R-squared  0.9979  S.D. dependent var  59.077
Log likelihood      -270.10  Durbin-Watson stat  0.4599
F-statistic         10588.2  Prob(F-statistic)   0.0000
------------------------------------------------------
```

Which of the following statements is **not** correct for this estimation?

(a) An error correction model was estimated. ○

(b) No conclusion about possible autocorrelation of the error terms can be made based on the Durbin-Watson statistic because it is a dynamic model. ○

(c) The long-term effect of a permanent increase in income is significantly greater than the short-term (immediate) effect. ○

(d) The null hypothesis that the immediate effect of a one-euro increase in income equals 90 cents must be rejected at the 5% level. ○

1.12 Non-Stationarity and Cointegration

1.12.1. Multiple Choice

Which of the following time series processes is covariance stationary, assuming that the error terms ε_t are always identically and independently normally distributed?

(a) $y_t = y_{t-1} + \varepsilon_t$ ○

(b) $y_t = 2 + 5t + \varepsilon_t$ ○

(c) $y_t = 1.5 + 0.8y_{t-1} + \varepsilon_t$ ○

(d) $y_t = 0.2 + 0.3y_{t-1} + 0.4t + \varepsilon_t$ ○

1.12.2. True or False

The process $y_t = \alpha + y_{t-1} + \varepsilon_t$ has an expected value $E(Y_t) = \alpha + tY_0$ and a variance $Var(y_t) = \sigma t^2$. Thus, it is a non-stationary process.

(a) True ○
(b) False ○

1.12.3. `True or False`

In an econometric error correction model, it is assumed that the short-term adjustment is weaker than the adjustment in the long-term relationship.

(a) True ○
(b) False ○

1.12.4. `Multiple Choice`

Which of the following tests is a procedure for testing the null hypothesis of non-stationarity of a time series?

(a) Dickey-Fuller test ○
(b) White test ○
(c) KPSS test ○
(d) Durbin-Watson test ○

1.12.5. `Completion`

(a) A time series whose expected value, variance, and (auto-)covariance are time-invariant is called ____________________.
(b) If the dynamics of a time series cannot be captured by an $AR(1)$ process but can instead be described by an $AR(p)$ process ($p > 1$), the ____________________ test is suitable for testing the null hypothesis of non-stationarity.
(c) If a long-term equilibrium relationship exists between at least two time series such that the non-stationary components of their trends cancel out, this is referred to as ____________________.

1.12.6. `Multiple Choice`

A method used to test for the cointegration of two time series is ...

(a) ... the Engle-Granger procedure ○
(b) ... the White test ○
(c) ... the Jarque-Bera test ○
(d) ... the Box-Jenkins method ○

1.12.7. `Completion`

(a) If $I(1)$ variables are cointegrated, an ____________________ ________ can be estimated to capture both dynamic adjustment processes and the parameters of the long-term relationship.
(b) According to the Granger ____________________ theorem, each cointegration relationship has a corresponding error correction model.
(c) If there is no causal relationship between two time series, a correlation between these two quantities is referred to as ____________________.

1.12.8. `True or False`

A regression of non-stationary level variables is only meaningful if the non-stationary components of their trends cancel each other out. Consequently, future levels of the processes may drift apart in the long run.

(a) True .... ○
(b) False .... ○

1.13 Diagnostics and Forecasting

1.13.1. `Multiple Choice`

Not a meaningful measure of forecast quality is ...

(a) ... the root of the mean squared deviation between forecast and realization. .... ○
(b) ... the mean absolute deviation between forecast and realization. .... ○
(c) ... the root of the sum of the products of forecast and realization divided by the number of forecasts considered. .... ○
(d) ... the proportion of forecasts with the same sign as the realization. .... ○

1.13.2. `Multiple Choice`

Which test or method **does not** allow a comparison of forecasting models?

(a) Chow test .... ○
(b) Diebold-Mariano test .... ○
(c) Mean absolute forecast error .... ○
(d) Theil's U .... ○

1.13.3. `True or False`

Using the linear regression model $y_t = \alpha + \beta y_t^p + \varepsilon_t$, where y_t is the actual realization and y_t^p the forecast at time t, it can be tested whether the forecast is unbiased on average and shows the same variation. Here, $\alpha < 0$ indicates an underestimation and $\alpha > 0$ an overestimation of the actual values.

(a) True .... ○
(b) False .... ○

1.13.4. `Completion`

(a) The forecast quality metric that expresses the forecast error of a model relative to the forecast error of a benchmark forecast is called ______________________.
(b) To select a forecast model, the time span for which data are available is divided into an estimation and a ______________ period.
(c) It is recommended to use the ______________________ test to examine whether the forecast quality of two models differs significantly.

1.13.5. `Multiple Choice`

To evaluate a forecasting model, Theil's U is calculated relative to a "naive" model. If the forecasting model performs better than the "naive" model, then Theil's U is …

(a) … less than zero. ○
(b) … greater than zero and less than one. ○
(c) … greater than one. ○
(d) … less than − 1.96 or greater than 1.96. ○

1.13.6. `True or False`

The mean forecast error should ideally be zero. In this case, one can assume that there is no systematic bias in the forecasts.

(a) True ○
(b) False ○

1.13.7. `Multiple Choice`

To evaluate the quality of a forecast, different metrics are used. Which of the following statements about such metrics is **not** correct?

(a) A value of Theil's U based on the Root Mean Squared Errors (RMSE) of the model compared to the RMSE of a benchmark model greater than 2 indicates a relatively good forecast. ○
(b) The mean forecast error (ME) should be close to zero for a good forecast. However, a mean forecast error of zero does not automatically imply a good forecast. ○
(c) For the mean absolute forecast error (MAE), the distribution of the forecast errors over several periods is irrelevant, whereas for the root mean squared error (RMSE), a few large errors lead to a higher value than many small errors that are equal in total. ○
(d) There are applications, such as in forecasting economic turning points, where the correct prediction of the direction of change is especially important. ○

Exercises 2

The questions provided in this chapter are suitable for an in-depth study of the corresponding topics. They include calculation and comprehension questions as well as many practical examples that require the interpretation of outputs generated using econometric software such as Eviews or R. Some of these questions have also been part of exams. Detailed sample solutions for some of these problems can be found in Chap. 5.

2.1 Tasks and Principles of Empirical Economic Research

2.1.1. The application of statistical/econometric methods is just one step in a typical empirical analysis. What steps does applied economic research consist of?

2.1.2. Name some tasks/goals of empirical economic research.

2.1.3. Methods of empirical economic research can be used to examine whether and to what extent income inequality affects economic growth. Explain why this is not sufficient to determine an optimal level of inequality.

2.2 Data Basis of Empirical Economic Research

2.2.1. In autumn 2020, the number of positive tests for the novel coronavirus rose rapidly. Due to this development, the Robert Koch Institute (RKI) warned of a critical situation at Christmas 2020. On October 1, 2020, there were 2,503 newly registered infections. On 7 November 2020, the number of new infections was 23,399.

P. Winker et al., *Exercise Book Empirical Economic Research and Econometrics*, https://doi.org/10.1007/978-3-662-72713-3_2

(a) Use a simple linear trend model to predict the number of new infections on Christmas Eve 2020 (December 24, 2020) and Easter 2021 (4 April 2021) based on the two observations provided above.

Hint: For calculating the linear trend, the increase in values per day is most important, which you can obtain, for example, by dividing the change in the numbers of infections by the number of days between.

(b) How do the forecasts change if you assume an exponential trend model?

Hint: Calculating an exponential trend is equivalent to calculating a linear trend for natural logarithms of the values.

(c) What risks of statistical extrapolation become apparent in this example?

2.2.2. Using the following examples, explain the individual steps from describing real-world phenomena to obtaining concrete data. What difficulties arise in operationalization or measurement in each case?

- gross domestic product
- foreign direct investment in Germany
- unemployment rate
- nominal interest rates

2.2.3. Data quality plays a crucial role in the practical implementation of research questions in empirical economic research. In this context, explain three characteristics that the data should have.

2.2.4. In the context of admissions to certain degree programs, it is often discussed whether the cognitive intelligence of applicants should be considered. However, cognitive intelligence is a complex psychological concept. Thus, there exists no simple, uniform, and universally accepted method for measuring cognitive intelligence. To at least approximate cognitive intelligence in the selection process, the following three measurement methods are proposed:

(a) A personal interview with a member of the selection committee.

(b) Answering a randomly selected question from a quiz show (e.g. "Who Wants to Be a Millionaire?").

(c) A standardized IQ test that can be taken on a laptop.

Evaluate each of the three measurement methods in terms of the criteria of objectivity, reliability, and validity.

2.2.5. Why is it difficult to make a concrete statement about the quality of specific data, for example, in the form of a quality index or rating?

2.2.6. Order the following variables according to their data quality as perceived by you and explain which shortcomings make you list them further down.

- registered unemployed for overall underemployment
- gross domestics product for value added in a country
- exchange rate
- turnover in the shadow economy

2.3 Data Processing

2.3.1. A standard approach to measuring consumer price development consists in observing the prices of goods and services in a so-called "basket of goods" to calculate a weighted price index for a given time period. Changes in this index over time are then interpreted as the inflation rate of consumer prices.

(a) What assumption regarding the weighting of goods and services in the basket of goods underlies the Laspeyres price index? What is meant by the term "basket effect" in this context?

(b) Describe the problem of measuring the development of consumer prices that arises from the fact that, especially for technological goods, observing the prices of the same product over longer periods is hardly possible. Describe in an illustrative way (a formal presentation is not expected) how this problem is addressed using the so-called "hedonic price indices".

(c) Does measuring consumer price inflation using hedonic price indices in the area of computers tend to result in higher or lower inflation rates? Briefly justify your answer. Describe a situation/an application in which this form of inflation measurement is not valid.

2.3.2. If consumer prices for private households in Germany are indexed based on 2020=100, one obtains the values for 2015–2024 as shown in Table 2.1.

(a) Rebase the index to the base year 2015=100.

(b) Use the newly calculated values to verify the validity of the following relationship:

$$P^{CPI}_{2020=100}(t) = \frac{P^{CPI}_{2015=100}(t) \cdot P^{CPI}_{2020=100}(2015)}{100}$$

(c) Calculate the annual inflation rate of consumer prices for the period 2015–2024.

2.3.3. From Table 2.2, you can extract the values for the following indices:

- **Former West Germany**: Unit labor costs (per hour) 1981–1991.
- **Germany**: Unit labor costs (per hour) 1991–2020.
- **Germany**: Unit labor costs (per hour) 2020–2024.

Indicate the base years for all series. Then change the base year of all series to 1991=100 and build an index series for the entire period.

Table 2.1 Consumer Price Index

Year	2015	2016	2017	2018	2019	2020	2021	2022	2023	2024
$P^{CPI}_{2020=100}$	94.5	95.0	96.4	98.1	99.5	100.0	103.1	110.2	116.7	119.3

Source: Federal Statistical Office; GENESIS-Online; Table: 61111-0001

Table 2.2 Indices of Unit Labor Costs

Year	$I^{FRG}_{1981=100}$	Year	$I^{G}_{2015=100}$	Year	$I^{G}_{2015=100}$	Year	$I^{G}_{2015=100}$	Year	$I^{G}_{2020=100}$
1981	100.0	1991	73.8	2001	86.0	2011	91.7	2021	99.7
1982	104.1	1992	78.8	2002	86.7	2012	94.7	2022	104.1
1983	104.9	1993	82.2	2003	87.9	2013	96.8	2023	111.0
1984	105.9	1994	82.8	2004	87.4	2014	98.0	2024	117.2
1985	107.6	1995	84.8	2005	87.0	2015	100.0		
1986	110.3	1996	85.1	2006	84.9	2016	101.1		
1987	113.4	1997	84.3	2007	84.6	2017	102.3		
1988	113.7	1998	84.4	2008	86.9	2018	105.1		
1989	114.5	1999	85.3	2009	93.0	2019	108.5		
1990	117.1	2000	86.1	2010	91.5	2020	113.0		
1991	121.4								

Source: German Council of Economic Experts and Federal Statistical Office; GENESIS-Online Database; Table: 81000-0017

Table 2.3 Index of Collectively Agreed Hourly Earnings (Including Bonuses)

Year	2015	2016	2017	2018	2019	2020	2021	2022	2023	2024
$I^{W}_{2020=100}$	88.3	90.1	92.7	95.1	97.7	100.0	101.4	102.8	105.4	109.9

Source: Federal Statistical Office; GENESIS-Online; Table: 62221-0001

2.3.4. The development of collectively agreed hourly earnings (including bonuses) for the overall economy can be described by the index $I^{W}_{2020=100}$ as shown in Table 2.3. Calculate the annual growth rates of hourly wages and compare your result with the growth rate to be calculated in exercise 2.3.2. c).

2.4 Economic Indicators

2.4.1. Keyword "Stable price level": Instinctively, it may seem plausible to define the goal of a stable price level as a situation in which an economy does not show aggregate price dynamics (inflation rate $\pi = 0$). However, this definition does not correspond to economic policy practice.

(a) Explain why monetary authorities such as the European Central Bank (ECB) instead consider a small positive inflation rate acceptable or even preferable. What is the inflation goal of the ECB?

(b) How is inflation generally measured? Describe verbally or formally the basic structure of an aggregate price index.

(c) In addition, explain the basket effect and the resulting problems in measuring the consumer price inflation rate.

2.4.2. Keyword “Employment level”:

(a) How does the Federal Employment Agency measure the official unemployment rate?

(b) How does the official unemployment rate differ from a labor market tightness index?

(c) Which of the two previously mentioned concepts do you consider more suitable for making statements about the overall labor market situation? Explain your reasoning.

2.4.3. In an online petition to the German Bundestag dated 22 May 2007, the following was proposed:

“The German Bundestag should decide that the Federal Statistical Office shall publish the official number of unemployed people in Germany. The number of unemployed persons should be defined as: the total number of unemployed or job-seeking people during the entire reporting period, including recipients of benefits under SGB III (unemployment benefit I), under SGB II (unemployment benefit II), job-seekers with or without benefits, or those participating in job opportunities, training, or other labor market policy measures.”

The justification of the petition includes the following.

“To decide which party to vote for in federal elections, citizens need reliable information about the successes or failures of the parties involved in government. For a large majority of citizens, it is of paramount importance how well the government tackles the problem of mass unemployment. [...] For example, individuals who participate in measures and are legally obligated to terminate the measure immediately if offered a job in the primary labor market are nevertheless not counted as unemployed in current statistics.”

(a) With respect to what use case does the petitioner consider the unemployment figures published by the Federal Employment Agency as conceptually unsuitable or of only limited validity?

(b) Do you agree with the petitioner’s assessment? Please briefly justify your answer.

(c) The number of unemployed people calculated according to the petitioner’s proposal would be higher or lower than the figures from the Federal Employment Agency? Briefly justify your answer.

2.4.4. Keyword “External economic balance”:

(a) Services balance, trade balance, current account balance, and capital account balance are terms that frequently appear in economic news.

i. Provide a short outline of the relationship between these parts of the balance of payments.

ii. With reference to the Federal Republic of Germany and based on your empirical knowledge, what sign would you expect for the respective balances of these sub-accounts in 2025?

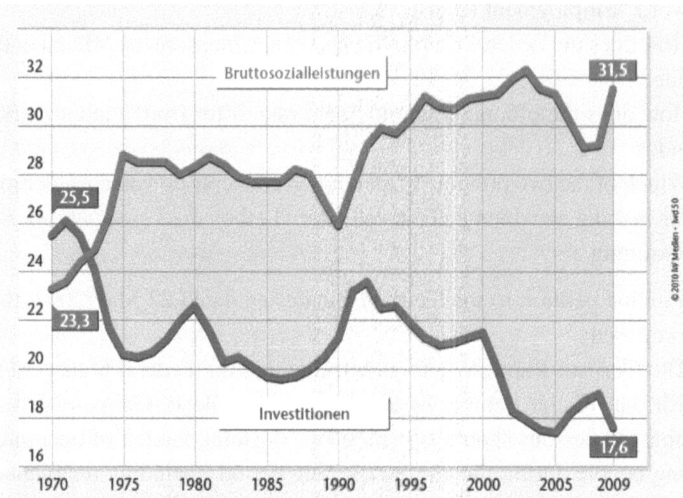

Fig. 2.1 Investments and social benefit shares. (Source: iwd 50/2010 p.1)

iii. Which balance do you personally consider the most suitable as an indicator of the external economic situation? Justify your response.

(b) Despite the popularity of the balance of payments, there are other indicators that can be used to describe the external economic situation. Name another indicator you consider suitable and explain it.

2.4.5. Keyword "Business cycle indicators":

(a) Which of the following proposed indicators do you consider suitable for determining the current economic situation? Justify your choice.

- Official unemployment rate
- Stock indices
- Production index of the manufacturing sector
- Index of incoming orders

(b) What aspects, in your opinion, argue against the use of the remaining proposed indicators?

(c) Explain the need to use indicators in business cycle analysis. What requirements should a suitable indicator meet?

2.4.6. Figure 2.1 is taken from an article in the information service of the German Economic Institute in Cologne. Thereby, "Bruttosozialleistungen" stands for gross social benefits shown in percent of GDP, while "Investitionen" is the share of investment in GDP (in percent).

(a) Explain how the two ratios presented in the figure differ conceptually.

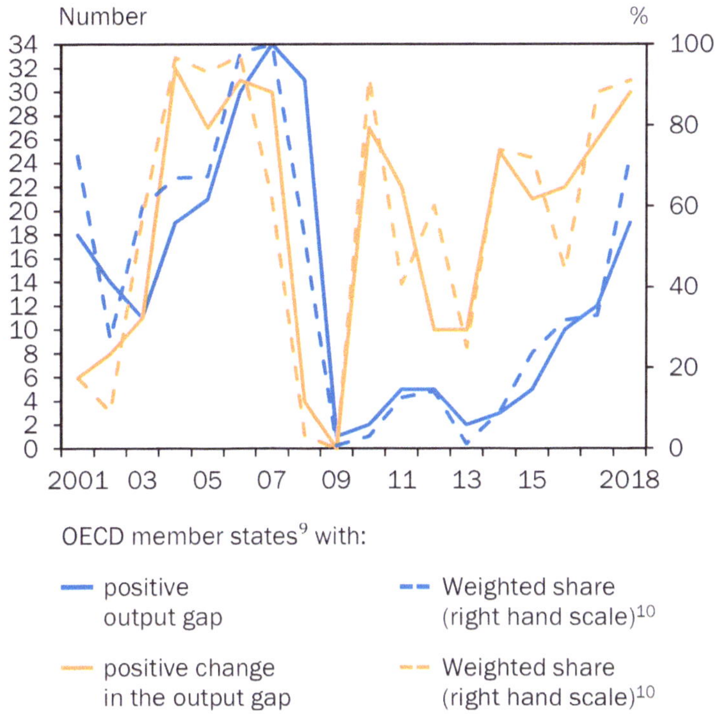

Fig. 2.2 Development of output gaps in OECD member countries. (Source: SVR 2018/19, p. 98)

(b) The heading of the figure in its original source was "Investments and social benefits: out of balance". Can this statement that a higher ratio of gross social benefits (compared to the investment ratio) represents a fundamental economic issue be supported solely based on the empirical findings? Explain your answer.

2.4.7. Figure 2.2 is taken from the 2018/19 Annual Report of the German Council of Economic Experts (https://www.sachverstaendigenrat-wirtschaft.de/fileadmin/dateiablage/gutachten/jg201819/Chapter_2.pdf).

The blue lines show the number or the GDP-weighted share of OECD countries with a positive output gap. The orange lines represent the corresponding numbers for positive changes. The output gap is defined as the relative deviation of GDP from the potential output.

(a) First, explain in general what a positive output gap indicates regarding a country's economic situation.
(b) How can the development in the number of positive output gaps since 2009 be interpreted? What phase of the business cycle does this indicate?

2.4.8. Figure 2.3 is taken from the ECB Report on financial structures (https://www.ecb.europa.eu/pub/pdf/other/reportonfinancialstructures201610.en.pdf, p. 30) and refers to the banking sector of the European Union (EU) and the Eurozone (EA).

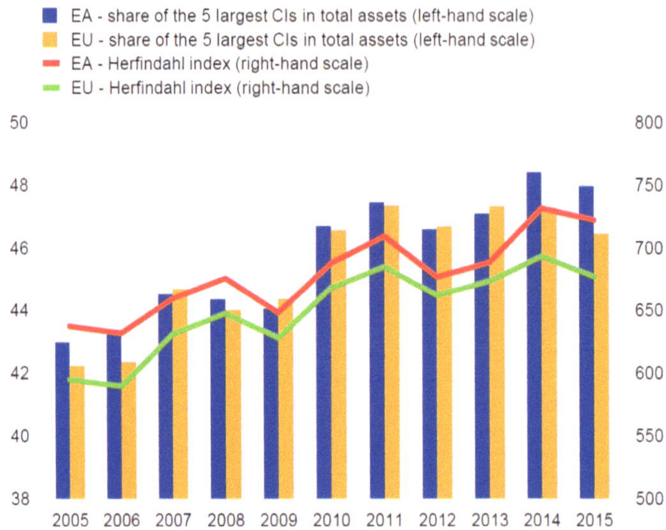

Fig. 2.3 Market concentration in the European banking system. (Source: ECB 2016, p. 30)

Fig. 2.4 Market concentration in the European banking system. (Source: ECB 2016, p. 30)

(a) Which of the displayed metrics represents the concentration rate CR_5 in the Eurozone?

(b) According to this measure, has concentration in the banking sector in the Eurozone increased between 2005 and 2015?

(c) Explain the concept of the Herfindahl index. Does its increase from 2005 to 2015 indicate an increase or a decrease in concentration in the banking sector?

2.4.9. Figure 2.4 is also taken from the ECB Report on financial structures (https://www.ecb.europa.eu/pub/pdf/other/reportonfinancialstructures201610.en.pdf, p. 30) and refers to the banking sector of the European Union (EU) and the Eurozone (EA).

(a) Describe the concept of the concentration rate CR_5 using the banking sector as an example, with bank assets as the relevant variable.

Fig. 2.5 Gini coefficient (%) for private wealth in Germany. (Source: DBB monthly report 4/2015, p. 54)

(b) How has the concentration rate CR_5 of credit institutions in Belgium (BE) and Germany (DE) developed between 2008 and 2015?

2.4.10. Figure 2.5 from the Monthly Report of the Deutsche Bundesbank (German Central Bank) (https://publikationen.bundesbank.de/publikationen-en/reports-studies/monthly-reports/monthly-report-april-2025-954672, p. 54) shows the development of the Gini coefficient for net private wealth in Germany from 2011 to 2024.

(a) Describe the idea of the Lorenz curve assuming that $w_1, \ldots, w_N$ denotes the wealth of N persons in Germany surveyed in a given year.

(b) How is the Gini coefficient obtained from a Lorenz curve?

(c) Provide a sketch of the Lorenz curve underlying the data for the last quarter of 2024 in Fig. 2.5. How would the Lorenz curve for the third quarter of 2014 differ?

(d) Would you expect that the Gini coefficient for net household income in Germany is larger or smaller than the one shown for wealth? Provide an argument for your suggestion.

2.4.11. Figure 2.6 comes also from the Deutsche Bundesbank Monthly Report (German Central Bank) (https://publikationen.bundesbank.de/publikationen-en/reports-

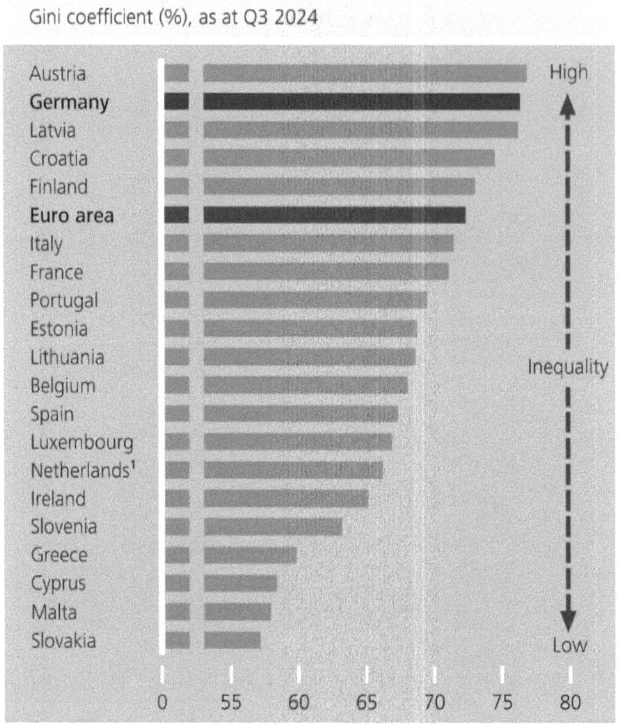

Fig. 2.6 Gini coefficient (%) for private wealth in Germany. (Source: DBB monthly report 4/2015, p. 54)

studies/monthly-reports/monthly-report-april-2025-954672, p. 54) and shows Gini coefficients for net private wealth for different countries in the Euro zone in 2024.

In the description of the data, it is mentioned that the underlying concept of wealth does not include entitlements to statutory pensions.

(a) Would you expect that the Gini coefficient for Germany would be lower if entitlement for statutory pensions were included in the wealth concept? Please provide a short explanation of your statement.

(b) Would you expect that the ranking of countries regarding wealth inequality would be different if such entitlements were taken into account for all countries? Please explain your argument,

2.5 Input-Output Analysis

2.5.1. On page 51 you will find an input-output (IO) table (Fig. 2.7) for three sectors of the German economy for 2021 (Revision 2024), provided by the German

National accounts, domestic product

Input-output-accounts

Input-output table 2021 (Revision 2024) at basic prices - domestic output and imports - Euro bn

Supply	Use					
	input of homogeneous braches				final uses of products	total uses of products
	primary sector[1]	secondary sector[2]	tertiary sector[3]	total		
Primary sector[1]	11.3	48.5	3.6	63.4	37.3	100.7
Secondary sector[2]	14.2	1,245.8	324.6	1,584.6	2,135.3	3,719.9
Tertiary sector[3]	13.7	554.5	1,460.0	2,028.2	2,569.0	4,597.2
Intermediate consumption of homogeneous branches and final uses of goods	39.2	1,848.8	1,788.2	3,676.2	4,741.6	8,417.8
Taxes on products less subsidies on products	1.7	22.0	81.4	105.0	283.2	388.2
Intermediate consumption of homogeneous branches and final uses of products at purchase prices	40.9	1,870.8	1,869.6	3,781.2	5,024.8	8,806.0
Compensation of employees (domestic concept)	7.7	499.1	1,456.2	1,963.0	X	X
Other taxes on production less other subsidies on production	- 6.0	- 24.8	- 50.8	- 81.6	X	X
Consumption of fixed capital	11.8	149.4	549.5	710.8	X	X
Net operating surplus	12.2	173.4	510.4	696.0	X	X
Gross value added	25.8	797.2	2,465.2	3,288.2	X	X
Output	66.7	2,668.0	4,334.8	7,069.5	X	X
↳ including: production for further processing	6.4	158.1	-	164.4	X	X
Imports of similar products at cost. insurance. freight (cif)-prices	34.1	1,051.9	262.4	1,348.3	X	X
↳ including: Imports of similar products from EU countries at cost. insurance. freight (cif)-prices	21.5	558.9	127.6	707.9	X	X
Total supply of products	100.7	3.719.9	4,597.2	8,417.8	X	X

1: Agriculture. forestry and fishing.
2: Industry.
3: Services.
X = Cell blocked for logical reasons.
- = No figures or magnitude zero.

As at 22 January 2025

Fig. 2.7 Input-Output Table 2021 (Revision 2024). (Source: Federal Statistical Office)

Federal Statistical Office (https://www.destatis.de/EN/Themes/Economy/National-Accounts-Domestic-Product/Tables/input-output-accounts.html).

(a) Use this example to explain the main idea and the general structure of an IO table. In particular, address the following aspects:

- The relationship between IO tables and the definitional equations of national accounts.
- The schematic structure of the respective quadrants.

(b) Show formally that the output values of all sectors (**X**) can be represented as a function of the components of the final demand (**Y**).

(c) The matrix of input coefficients (rounded) in the given example is as follows (rounded to two decimal places):

$$\mathbf{A} = \begin{pmatrix} 0.11 & 0.01 & 0.00 \\ 0.14 & 0.33 & 0.07 \\ 0.14 & 0.15 & 0.32 \end{pmatrix}.$$

- What fundamental assumption characterizes the matrix **A** in the Leontief model?
- Discuss this assumption from an economic perspective: How can this assumption be justified, and why can it also be criticized?
- Calculate the Leontief inverse corresponding to **A** (again rounded to two decimal places).

(d) A fictitious example on the topic of "structural change": Suppose that the total output of goods in the primary sector is to be reduced by -1.0 billion euros, while that of the tertiary sector is to be increased by $+1.0$ billion euros, with the total output of goods in the secondary sector remaining unchanged, i.e.: $\Delta\mathbf{X} = \begin{pmatrix} -1 & 0 & 1 \end{pmatrix}'$. What changes to the final demand vector would be necessary to induce the desired total effect?

(e) Suppose that the final demand for goods from the tertiary sector increases autonomously by 50 billion euros (that is, $\Delta\mathbf{Y}_3 = 50$): How would this affect the production volumes of all sectors **X**?

2.5.2. Use the simplified input-output table in Table 2.4 to answer the following questions.

(a) Interpret intermediate inputs $V_{1,1}$ and $V_{2,1}$, where $V_{i,j}$ denotes intermediate inputs delivered by sector i to sector j. Provide a relevant example of goods or services that are considered intermediate inputs in $V_{1,1}$ and $V_{2,1}$, respectively.

(b) Calculate and interpret the output coefficients $b_{1,1}$, $b_{1,2}$, and $b_{1,4}$, where $1, 2, 3$ corresponds to the production sectors and 4 to the final demand.

Table 2.4 Simplified Input-Output Table

	Agriculture	Industry	Services	Final Demand	Total
Agriculture	20	4	7	19	50
Industry	11	40	12	37	100
Services	5	32	42	41	120
Labor	14	24	59		
Total	50	100	120		

(c) Calculate and interpret the input coefficients $a_{1,2}$, $a_{2,1}$, and $a_{4,1}$, where 4 refers to the labor factor in the fourth row of the input-output table.
(d) Describe the matrix A needed to calculate the Leontief inverse $(I - A)^{-1}$. You do not need to compute each element of the matrix; it is sufficient to clarify which elements the matrix contains.

2.6 The Econometric Model

2.6.1. List relevant steps in setting up and interpreting an econometric model.

2.6.2. Describe the concept of an econometric model and illustrate the terms "dependent variable", "explanatory variable", "functional form", and "error term" using an example of your choice.

2.6.3. Why is the error term in an econometric model of great importance? What properties of the model can be inferred from it (or based on the estimated residuals)?

2.7 The Linear Regression Model

2.7.1. The Research Data Centers for Official Statistics in Germany provide anonymized data on the 2001 income tax statistics[1]. These data include, among other things, information on income and levied income tax. On this basis, you want to estimate the marginal tax rate (marginal tax) for taxpayers in tax class I (singles) with income below €200,000.

Discuss why the initially plausible model

$$\text{Tax}_i = \beta_0 + \beta_1 \text{Income}_i + \varepsilon_i$$

might not be the best choice.

When sticking to the model and estimating it with the available data, what would be your estimator of the marginal tax rate based on this model? Propose an alternative specification for the model and explain how the marginal tax rate would be obtained in this case.

2.7.2. This task is based on exercise 2.7 in Wooldridge (2008), "Introductory Econometrics—A Modern Approach", 5th ed., p. 63: In their 1995 paper (Kiel and McClain, "The Effect of Incinerator Siting on Housing Appreciation Rates", Journal of Urban Economics 37, 311–323, http://www.sciencedirect.com/science/article/pii/S0094119085710169), the authors examined the relationship between

[1] http://www.forschungsdatenzentrum.de/de/10-21242-73111-2001-00-00-5-1-0

housing prices and distance to a new incinerator, using data on home sales in Andover, Massachusetts in 1988. Based on $N = 134$ observations, they obtained the following estimates:

$$\widehat{lnP} = 9.40 + 0.321 lnD .$$

Here, the variables are denoted:

lnP: Natural logarithm of house price
lnD: Natural logarithm of distance to the incinerator

(a) Interpret the coefficient of lnD. Does the sign of the estimated coefficient match your expectations?
(b) In your opinion, can it be assumed that this simple regression analysis provides an unbiased estimate of the elasticity of P with respect to D? Consider in your reasoning how the city administration might have made its decision on the location of the incinerator.
(c) The estimation reports an R^2 of 0.162. What conclusion can be derived from this value about the estimated relationship?
(d) What other factors might influence the price of a house? Could these factors be partially correlated with the distance from the incinerator?

2.7.3. Explain the principle of least squares estimation and its properties. In particular, address the following aspects:
(a) Describe in your own words how the parameters of an econometric model can be estimated by the least squares method (a formal presentation is not required).
(b) Name three properties that an OLS estimator can have and explain why these are desirable for empirical analysis.
(c) What assumptions must be met for the OLS estimator to possess all the desired properties mentioned in (b)?

2.7.4. Show that from the general formula for the OLS estimator $\hat{\beta} = \left(X'X\right)^{-1} X'y$, the following solution results for the special case with one explanatory variable x and a constant:

$$\hat{\beta}_1 = \bar{y} - \hat{\beta}_2\bar{x} \text{ and } \hat{\beta}_2 = \frac{\overline{xy} - \bar{x}\bar{y}}{\overline{x^2} - \bar{x}^2} .$$

2.7.5. The following figure shows the result of a least squares estimation for German data using EViews. The variables denote:[2]

[2] This task uses seasonally adjusted data to keep the presentation concise. Disregard this characteristic in your response.

CONSUMPTION: Private consumption in billion euros at current prices
DISP_INCOME: Disposable income in billion euros at current prices

```
Dependent Variable: CONSUMPTION    Method: Least Squares
Sample: 1991:1 2020:4          Included observations: 120
--------------------------------------------------------
Variable     Coefficient  Std. Error   t-Statistic  Prob.
--------------------------------------------------------
C              2.048156     4.797358      0.426934   0.6702
DISP_INCOME   0.886359     0.012614      70.26688   0.0000
--------------------------------------------------------
R-squared            0.9767    Mean dependent var   333.24
Adjusted R-squared 0.9764    S.D. dependent var   63.805
--------------------------------------------------------
```

(a) Write down the estimated regression model using the usual notation.
(b) Interpret the coefficient of the variable DISP_INCOME.
(c) Based on the estimation results reported, can you reject the null hypothesis (at the 5% level) that the effect of this variable (DISP_INCOME) is actually equal to one?
(d) What does the reported R^2 statistic measure? How should the given value be interpreted?

2.7.6. The following output shows the result of a least squares estimation using EViews. The variables denote:
TAX : Levied income tax in euros in 2001
INCOME : Income in euros in 2001

```
Dependent Variable: TAX             Method: Least Squares
Included observations: 89963
--------------------------------------------------------
Variable     Coefficient  Std. Error t-Statistic   Prob.
--------------------------------------------------------
C             -1485.182     5.280610   -281.2520  0.0000
INCOME         0.230622     0.000307    750.9454  0.0000
INCOME^2       1.40E-06     3.24E-09    433.3426  0.0000
--------------------------------------------------------
R-squared             0.9810  Mean dependent var 4210.319
Adjusted R-squared 0.9810  S.D. dependent var 5826.464
--------------------------------------------------------
```

Only observations with income between 0 and 200,000 euros in 2001 were included. Moreover, only taxpayers in tax class I (singles) were considered. The entry `1.40E-06` represents the value $1.4 \cdot 10^{-6}$. Similarly, `3.24E-09` represents $3.24 \cdot 10^{-9}$.

(a) Write down the estimated regression model using the usual notation.
(b) What is the expected income tax for a taxpayer with an income of € 100,000 in 2001?
(c) Interpret the coefficient of the variable `INCOME^2`.
(d) Based on the estimation results reported, can you reject the null hypothesis (at level 5%) that the effect of this variable (`INCOME^2`) is actually zero? What substantive conclusion follows from the result?
(e) What does the reported R^2 statistic measure? How should the given value be interpreted?

2.7.7. The following output shows the result of a least squares estimation using EViews for Swiss data. The variables denote:
`LOG(M3)` : The natural logarithm of the money supply (i.e., $ln(M3)$)
`LOG(P)` : The natural logarithm of the price level
(measured by the GDP deflator P)

```
Dependent Variable: LOG(M3)       Method: Least Squares
Sample: 1985Q1 2024Q3         Included observations: 159
-------------------------------------------------------
Variable  Coefficient  Std. Error  t-Statistic    Prob.
-------------------------------------------------------
C           -3.368536    0.744864    -4.522347   0.0000
LOG(P)       3.677464    0.164284     22.38475   0.0000
-------------------------------------------------------
R-squared             0.7614  Mean dependent var 13.30048
Adjusted R-squared 0.7599  S.D. dependent var 0.449626
-------------------------------------------------------
```

(a) Write down the estimated regression model using the usual notation.
(b) Interpret the coefficient of the variable `LOG(P)`. Which conclusion does the coefficient allow for the relationship between the money supply (M3) and the GDP-deflator (P)?
(c) Is the constant in the model (C) statistically significant different from 0 at significance level 5%?
(d) Do you have to reject the null hypothesis that the coefficient of `LOG(P)` is different from 3 at the 5% level?

2.7.8. You are examining the question of how an increase in the number of police officers affects the crime rate. For this purpose, you have data from 92 U.S. counties. You estimate the following regression model:

$$\text{CRMRTE}_i = \beta_1 + \beta_2 \text{POLPC}_i + \varepsilon_i .$$

The variables are defined as follows:
`CRMRTE` : Crime rate (number of offenses per 1 000 inhabitants)
`POLPC` : Number of police officers per 1 000 inhabitants
The following figure shows the estimation results using EViews.

```
Dependent Variable: CRMRTE        Method: Least Squares
Included observations: 92
------------------------------------------------------
Variable  Coefficient  Std. Error  t-Statistic   Prob.
------------------------------------------------------
C            61.79782     10.83483     5.703625  0.0000
POLPC        17.31683     4.634848     3.736223  0.0003
------------------------------------------------------
R-squared              0.1343  Mean dependent var 100.7908
Adjusted R-squared 0.1247  S.D. dependent var 29.84309
------------------------------------------------------
```

(a) Interpret the coefficients reported for `C` and `POLPC`.
(b) What recommendation would you make to a policy maker based on the results?
(c) How would you assess the results of the regression analysis in general?

2.8 Residual Analysis and Check of Model Assumptions

2.8.1. The following figure shows the result of an ordinary least squares estimation with EViews for a money demand function for Germany.
The following variables are used:
`LOG(M3)` : Natural logarithm of the money supply M3
`LOG(GDP)` : Natural logarithm of GDP
`LOG(R)` : Natural logarithm of the money market interest rate
The variables `M3` and `GDP` were recalculated for the period before reunification, so that no structural break was present in 1990.3.

```
Dependent Variable: LOG(M3)        Method: Least Squares
Sample: 1972:1 1998:4        Included observations: 108
------------------------------------------------------
Variable   Coefficient  Std. Error  t-Statistic  Prob.
------------------------------------------------------
C            -0.288753    0.035055    -8.237251  0.0000
LOG(GDP)      1.189971    0.020915     56.89447  0.0000
LOG(R)       -0.017045    0.003037    -5.612655  0.0000
------------------------------------------------------
R-squared            0.9795 Mean dependent var    1.9529
Adjusted R-squared 0.9791 S.D. dependent var      0.0419
S.E. of regression 0.0060 Akaike info criterion -7.351
Sum squared resid  0.0038 Schwarz criterion      -7.276
Log likelihood   399.9477 F-statistic           2509.494
Durbin-Watson stat 1.3701 Prob(F-statistic)       0.0000
------------------------------------------------------
```

(a) Write down the estimated regression model using the usual notation.

(b) Interpret the coefficient for the variable LOG(GDP). Does the value of this variable meet your expectations?

(c) What does the Durbin-Watson statistic measure? How should the reported value of this statistic be interpreted?

(d) What reason might have led the authors to limit the analysis to the period up to the end of 1998?

2.8.2. For various tests (e.g. t–test and F–test), it is assumed that the actual error terms are independent realizations of a normal distribution with zero mean and constant variance.

(a) Explain possible consequences for the interpretation of an estimation result if these conditions are not met.

(b) Describe a method to check whether the assumption of normal distribution of the error terms is met.

(c) Describe a method to check whether the assumption of constant variance of the error terms is met.

(d) Describe a method to check whether the assumption of independence is met.

(e) What causes may be responsible for dependence of the error terms over time? Name at least two possible causes and explain how they can lead to autocorrelation.

2.8.3. For the estimation shown in Exercise 2-7-6, additional test statistics were calculated.

(a) First, a value of 1.73 was reported for the Durbin-Watson statistic. What property of the error terms does this test statistic examine? Does its application make sense in the specific application setting? What conclusion does the test statistic allow?

(b) In a second step, the Jarque-Bera statistic was calculated for the residuals of the estimated model. Its value is $2.82 \cdot 10^9$. What conclusion does this result allow? Provide the null hypothesis of the test, the test result and the implication for the specific application.

(c) Finally, another test was conducted. The following output shows the test equation estimated for this test. What test has been conducted? What is the null hypothesis? Which of the reported pieces of information represents the test statistic? Does the null hypothesis has to be rejected?

```
Test Equation:
Dependent Variable: RESID^2      Method: Least Squares
Included observations: 89963
-----------------------------------------------------
Variable  Coefficient  Std. Error  t-Statistic  Prob.
-----------------------------------------------------
C              3614573.   164347.2    21.99352  0.0000
INCOME       -675.7331   20.51527   -32.93806  0.0000
INCOME^2      0.029661   0.000720    41.17570  0.0000
INCOME*(INCOME^2)
             -3.99E-07   8.20E-09   -48.60715  0.0000
(INCOME^2)^2  1.62E-12   2.76E-14    58.57315  0.0000
-----------------------------------------------------
R-squared           0.1262 Mean dependent var   644902
Adjusted R-squared 0.1262 S.D. dependent var   190152
S.E. of regression 177753 Akaike info criter.  36.225
Sum squared resid 2.8E+19 Schwarz criterion    36.225
Log likelihood    -1629431 Hannan-Quinn criter. 36.225
F-statistic        3247.95 Durbin-Watson stat   0.2683
-----------------------------------------------------
```

2.8.4. The following output provides the results of a regression analysis based on data from the World Happiness Report 2021 (https://worldhappiness.report/). The World Happiness Report is a report on the state of global happiness that has been published annually since 2012 and allows for a comparison of countries by happiness level. The happiness values and rankings are based on data from the Gallup World Poll. The values of the `HAPPINESS SCORE` are based on responses to the question "How would you rate your happiness on a scale from 0 to 10, where 10 represents the highest happiness?"

The present regression is based on a cross-sectional analysis for 126 countires in the year 2019. It should help to assess the impact of six factors in explaining the happiness index: The logarithm of GDP per capita (LOG_GDP), social support (SOCIAL_SUPPORT), healthy life expectancy at birth (LIFE_EXPECTANCY), freedom to make life choices (FREEDOM), perceptions of corruption (CORRUPTION), and generosity (GENEROSITY).

```
Dependent Variable: HAPPINESS SCORE
Included observations: 126        Method: Least Squares
------------------------------------------------------
Variable     Coefficient  Std. Error t-Statistic  Prob.
------------------------------------------------------
C                -2.2396     0.7444     -3.0084   0.0032
LOG_GDP           0.1253     0.1080      1.1609   0.2480
SOCIAL_SUPPORT   3.1616      0.7125      4.4370   0.0000
LIFE_EXPECTANCY 0.0506       0.0157      3.2122   0.0017
FREEDOM           1.6440     0.5539      2.9679   0.0036
CORRUPTION       -0.7261     0.3358     -2.1621   0.0326
GENEROSITY        0.3755     0.3812      0.9851   0.3266
------------------------------------------------------
R-squared            0.741424  Mean dependent var 5.55939
F-statistic          56.86867  Durbin-Watson stat 1.62799
Prob(F-statistic) 0.000000
------------------------------------------------------
```

(a) Please interpret the coefficients for LOG_GDP and LIFE_EXPECTANCY.
(b) Interpret the Durbin-Watson statistic.
(c) Figure 2.8 shows a scatterplot for SOCIAL_SUPPORT and residuals (RESID) of the above regression. What conclusions regarding properties of the error terms can be drawn from this plot?
(d) A White test was also performed. Interpret the result of the test. What conclusions would you draw from this test result?

```
------------------------------------------------------
Heteroskedasticity Test: White
Null hypothesis: Homoskedasticity
------------------------------------------------------
F-statistic             3.123  Prob. F(6,119)       0.0071
Obs*R-squared          17.140  Prob. Chi-Square(6) 0.0088
Scaled explained SS 21.359  Prob. Chi-Square(6) 0.0016
------------------------------------------------------
```

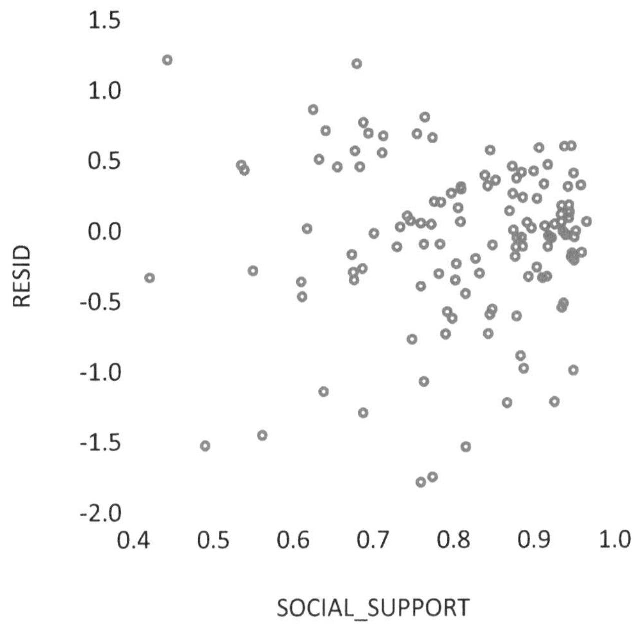

Fig. 2.8 Scatterplot for social support and residuals

2.9 Qualitative Variable

2.9.1. A linear regression model is used to examine whether, in addition to the duration of school education (SCHOOL) and the age (AGE), the type of employment relationship also has an influence on the salary level for full-time employees (WAGE). For this purpose, values are also available for three dummies: WORKER, EMPLOYEE, and OFFICIAL. These dummy variables each take the value one if a corresponding employment relationship exists, otherwise zero. For all persons in the sample exactly one of the three dummies takes on the value one.

When attempting to estimate the linear regression model

$$\begin{aligned} \texttt{WAGE}_i &= \alpha_0 + \alpha_1 \texttt{SCHOOL}_i + \alpha_2 \texttt{AGE}_i \\ &\quad + \alpha_3 \texttt{WORKER}_i + \alpha_4 \texttt{EMPLOYEE}_i + \alpha_5 \texttt{OFFICIAL}_i + \varepsilon_i \end{aligned}$$

the software provides the error message "near singular matrix".

(a) Why can the model not be estimated in this form? Provide the term for the problem and explain it conceptually.

(b) How would the regression model need to be modified in order to quantify the relationships of interest?

2.9.2. The following output shows the result of a regression analysis based on data from the GSOEP 2019.

```
Dependent Variable: WAGE          Method: Least Squares
Included observations: 16243
-------------------------------------------------------
Variable    Coefficient  Std. Error  t-Statistic  Prob.
-------------------------------------------------------
C              3852.731     276.683       13.925   0.0000
DABI           2163.301     536.276       -4.465   0.0000
DSEX          -1809.480     405.231        4.304   0.0000
DABI*DSEX     -1074.173     764.727       -1.405   0.1601
-------------------------------------------------------
```

WAGE indicates the gross monthly wage of the individuals considered. The dummy variable DABI takes the value one if the person has obtained the highest school leaving degree (Abitur), otherwise zero. DSEX takes the value one for women, otherwise zero.

(a) What is the resulting average (expected) income for men and women with and without the Abitur?
(b) How do you interpret the coefficient for the term DABI*DSEX?
(c) How does the average income differ between women and men under the assumption that the proportion of men and women among the employed is equal and that 40% of women and 10% of men have obtained the Abitur?

2.9.3. The following output shows the result of the estimation of a consumption function for Germany, where CONSUMPTION denotes private consumption and DISP_INCOME denotes disposable income. Up to the end of 1990, the data refer to West Germany; from the beginning of 1991, to unified Germany. The dummy variable D91 takes the value zero until the end of 1990 and one thereafter. In addition to the constant C, three seasonal dummies were also estimated. For clarity, the coefficients of the seasonal dummies are not shown here.

```
Dependent Variable: CONSUMPTION  Method: Least Squares
Sample: 1960Q1 2020Q4        Included observations: 244
Variable    Coefficient  Std. Error  t-Statistic  Prob.
-------------------------------------------------------
C              2.042447    1.286577     1.587505   0.1137
DISP_INCOME    0.885746    0.010240     86.50209   0.0000
D91            1.894200    3.024447     0.626296   0.5317
D91*DISP_INCOME
0.000482      0.012637    0.038147    0.9696
-------------------------------------------------------
```

(a) What would the estimated marginal propensity to consume be if only the data for West Germany up to and including 1990 were used?
(b) Accordingly, what would be the estimated marginal propensity to consume for the all-German data from 1991 onward?
(c) Is the difference in the estimated marginal propensities to consume statistically significant? Justify your response. What economic reasons could be decisive for the result?

2.9.4. Using a suitable example, explain the linear probability model. Thereby, explain possible advantages and disadvantages of this approach.

2.9.5. Briefly illustrate the difference between probit and logit models. Furthermore, discuss the potential advantages of these methods compared to the linear probability model.

2.9.6. The following output shows the result of estimating a probit model using EViews.

```
Dependent Variable: ABITUR  Method: ML - Binary Probit
Sample: 1 17646             Included observations: 17646
Convergence achieved after 3 iterations
-------------------------------------------------------
Variable  Coefficient  Std. Error  z-Statistic  Prob.
-------------------------------------------------------
C           -0.419506    0.014058    -29.84167   0.0000
GENDER      -0.223907    0.019926    -11.23693   0.0000
-------------------------------------------------------
```

The following variables are used:

`ABITUR` : Dummy variable: 1 if individual i has achieved the highest school leaving degree (Abitur), 0 otherwise
`GENDER` : Gender: 1 for women, 0 for other

(a) Provide a formal representation of the estimated model. Which components of the model must be estimated and how can the probability of obtaining the Abitur be calculated?
(b) How are the estimated coefficients to be interpreted? Are there differences compared to interpreting the results of an OLS estimation? If so, why?
(c) What is the difference between a probit and a logit model?

2.9.7. Table 2.5 shows a small excerpt from the estimation results of a probit model presented by N. Barasinska and D. Schäfer in Discussion Paper 05/2013 of the Deutsche Bundesbank. The dependent variable `Risky` takes the value zero if the individual does not hold risky assets (equity funds), and one if he or she does hold such assets.

Table 2.5 Estimation results from Marasinska and Schäfer (2013, p. 15)

	Italy
	(1)
Male	0.087***
	(0.016)
ln(Income)	0.117***
	(0.016)
II Wealth quartile	0.191
	(0.145)
III Wealth quartile	0.262**
	(0.13)
IV Wealth quartile	0.286***
	(0.084)
Real Property	0.023
	(0.019)
Self-Employed	−0.013***
	(0.022)
Education	0.109***
	(0.026)
...	...
Pseudo-R^2	0.13
AIC	2556
BIC	2651
Number of obs.	2806

Note: *p <0.1; **p <0.05; ***p <0.01

The results shown here refer to data from Italy. `Male` is a dummy variable taking the value one for men and zero otherwise; `ln(Income)` is the natural logarithm of the individual's income; the dummies `II Wealth quartile`, `III Wealth quartile`, and `IV Wealth quartile` indicate membership in the respective wealth quartile; the dummy `Real Property` denotes real estate ownership; the dummy `Self-Employed` identifies self-employed individuals; and the dummy `Education` indicates a higher educational degree. The equation includes additional explanatory variables that are not shown here. For each variable, the marginal effect is reported for the situation when all variables take on the national average.

Below the estimated marginal effects, the estimated standard errors are reported in parentheses. The asterisks $***$ and $**$ indicate that the null hypothesis of a true marginal effect of zero can be rejected at the significance levels 1% and 5%, respectively.

(a) What can be said about the influence of the variable `Male`?

(b) What does the marginal effect of 0.117 for the variable `ln(Income)` imply about the impact of a 1% increase in income on the probability of holding risky assets?

(c) What conclusions can be drawn from the results for the three dummy variables `II Wealth quartile`, `III Wealth quartile`, and `IV Wealth quartile`?

2.9.8. Critically discuss the statement: "The estimated marginal effects in the linear probability model and the probit model are identical."

2.9.9. In the study by V.R. Rao and E.W. McLaughlin, "Modeling the Decision to Add New Products by Channel Intermediaries" (Journal of Marketing, 53, 1998, 80–88), the authors investigate which factors influence the decision of retail chains to introduce new products. Based on theoretical considerations, several relevant factors were identified. Data were collected weekly over half a year from a medium-sized retail chain in the U.S. and its suppliers. The empirical analysis is based on 2,034 individual decisions, in 31.9% of which the new product was introduced. Due to missing values, 687 observations remained for the econometric analysis.

Table 2.6 presents some results from the estimation of a logit model. Note that the coefficients are followed by χ^2 statistics in parentheses. The more commonly used t-statistic can be obtained by taking the square root of the χ^2 statistic while preserving the sign of the coefficient. For example, the t-statistic for the constant `(Intercept)` is $-\sqrt{41.92} = -6.47$.

Answer the following questions based on the results shown in the table.

(a) Is the influence of the gross margin (`Gross margin`) on the probability of listing the product positive or negative? Does the result align with theoretical expectations? Is the effect significantly different from zero at the 5% level? Please briefly explain your answer.

(b) Can the results be directly interpreted to determine by how many percentage points the probability of listing the product increases if the gross margin doubles? Please briefly explain your answer.

(c) The paper also presents Table 2.7. Explain the entries in the table. How would the table look like in case the model predicts the actual outcome for all observations?

2.10 Trend and Seasonal Adjustment

2.10.1. Keyword "HP-Filter"

(a) Let X_t denote the time series under consideration. Then the HP trend component H_t is obtained by solving the optimization problem:

$$\min_{H_1 \ldots H_T} \sum_{t=1}^{T} (X_t - H_t)^2 + \lambda \sum_{t=2}^{T-1} [(H_{t+1} - H_t) - (H_t - H_{t-1})]^2$$

Table 2.6 Logit model on the determinants of product introductions, Source: Rao and McLaughlin (1998, p. 85)

Group of items variable	All items[a]	
Intercept	−5.47	(41.92)[b]
Gross margin	−.06	(10.30)[b]
Profit per shelf volume	.004	(3.24)[c]
Opportunity cost	−.001	(1.14)[c]
Number of competing firms	.14	(11.72)[b,c]
Number of competing brands	−.03	(1.89)[c]
Product uniqueness	.25	(18.03)[b,c]
Vendor effort	.03	(.46)[c]
Terms of trade dummies		
Off-invoice	−.19	(.70)[c]
Slotting allowance	−.43	(2.03)[c]
Billback	−.93	(6.04)[b,c]
Free cases	−.22	(.87)
Low price dummy	−.17	(.30)
Medium price dummy	.02	(.01)[c]
Expected category growth	.68	(46.49)[b,c]
Synergy dummy	−.31	(2.01)[c]
Product category dummies	See Table 2.4	
Number of observations	687	
Model chi square, d.f.	249.49, 23	
P-value	0.0	

[a] Entries are coefficient and chi square for each variable (with 1 d.f.)
[b] Significant at .05 level
[c] Sign of the coefficient is according to expectations

Table 2.7 Model Fit

	Prediction		
Actual	Accepted	Rejected	Total
Accepted	125	98	223
Rejected	51	413	464
Total	176	511	687

- Explain the basic idea and key property of the Hodrick–Prescott (HP) filter based on the objective function in the minimization problem.
- What role does the parameter λ play in this context? How would the characteristics of H_t change when increasing or decreasing the value of λ, respectively?

(b) Describe the "endpoint problem" of the application of the HP-filter and its impact on empirical analysis.

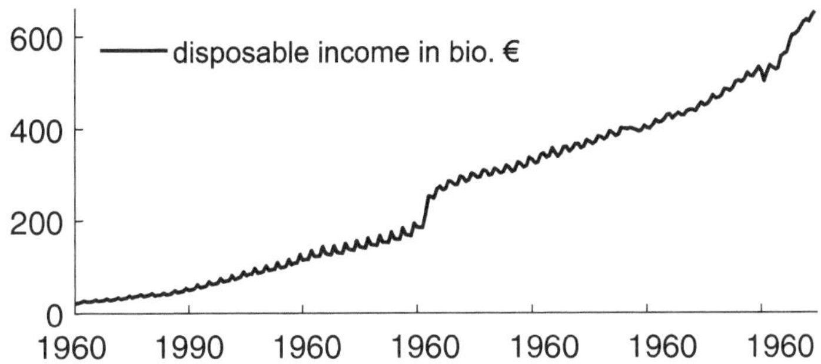

Fig. 2.9 Disposable income in Germany 1960–2020. (Source: Data from Federal Statistical Office of Germany; GENESIS-Online Database, Table: 81000-0005; own illustration)

2.10.2. Figure 2.9 shows a time series plot of the disposable income of private households in Germany from 1960 to 2020 (you may ignore the obvious structural break when answering the following questions).

(a) When considering only the period up to 1990, would you prefer an additive or multiplicative approach to decomposing this series into its basic components? Justify your response.

(b) Describe formally how your preferred approach is to be implemented.

(c) Based on this specific example, name a relevant criticism that might question the suitability of performing a component decomposition in this case.

2.10.3. Keyword "Regression with seasonal dummies": One way of obtaining seasonal adjustment consists in using a linear regression with the so-called "seasonal dummies". As an example, refer to the output shown below, which presents the results of such an approach for the time series of the monthly total index of German retail sales (price adjusted, excluding motor vehicles). The variable `@SEAS(M)` stands for a dummy taking on the value 1 in month `M` and zero else.

```
Dep. Variable: RETAIL_INDex_REAL Method: Least Squares
Sample: 2008M01 2025M04      Included observations: 208
-----------------------------------------------------
Variable  Coefficient  Std. Error  t-Statistic  Prob.
-----------------------------------------------------
@SEAS(1)     95.58889    2.226067     42.94071    0.0000
@SEAS(2)     92.63333    2.226067     41.61301    0.0000
@SEAS(3)     105.9389    2.226067     47.59016    0.0000
@SEAS(4)     103.7611    2.226067     46.61186    0.0000
@SEAS(5)     103.6294    2.290604     45.24109    0.0000
@SEAS(6)     102.2353    2.290604     44.63246    0.0000
@SEAS(7)     104.3294    2.290604     45.54668    0.0000
@SEAS(8)     100.8941    2.290604     44.04695    0.0000
```

```
@SEAS(9)      101.1647    2.290604    44.16508    0.0000
@SEAS(10)     106.8647    2.290604    46.65351    0.0000
@SEAS(11)     110.3588    2.290604    48.17892    0.0000
@SEAS(12)     120.8882    2.290604    52.77570    0.0000
--------------------------------------------------------
R-squared          0.3569   Mean dependent var   103.9365
Adj. R-squared 0.3208   S.D. dependent var    11.45939
--------------------------------------------------------
```

(a) Describe the formal approach: Provide the formula for the estimated equation, where you might use y_t to describe the retail sales variable and $s_{M,t}$ for the seasonal dummy for month M. What assumption about the seasonal pattern is made implicitly when using this model?
(b) Are the coefficients for seasonal dummies statistically significant (i.e., different from zero)? Can anything be inferred about the relevance (in the statistical sense) of seasonal effects based on the available output?
(c) A graphical comparison of the original time series, the values predicted by the seasonal dummies (upper part) and the estimated residuals (lower part) can be found in Fig. 2.10. Describe the plots provided in the figure by focusing on the success of the model in reflecting the seasonal pattern of the data.

2.10.4. In an analysis by the Deutsche Bundesbank for monthly data (1999–2006), the time series for a stock index s_t (Stoxx 50) was used to calculate the series of continuously compounded annual returns, i.e., $\Delta^{12}s_t = \ln(s_t) - \ln(s_{t-12})$, which were then used in further econometric analysis.
(a) First, state the advantage of using annual growth rates or annual returns when dealing with higher-frequency data.
(b) Estimating the model $\Delta^{12}s_t = \beta_1 + \beta_2\Delta^{12}s_{t-1} + \varepsilon_t$ yielded a statistically significant estimate for β_2 with a value of 0.944. Can this result be interpreted as evidence of autocorrelation in stock returns, i.e., that past values can predict future developments? How can the high and significant value of $\hat{\beta}_2$ be explained?
(c) Instead, when considering monthly returns, defined as $\Delta s_t = \ln(s_t) - \ln(s_{t-1})$, the estimation of the model $\Delta s_t = \beta_1 + \beta_2\Delta s_{t-1} + \varepsilon_t$ does not produce a significant effect for β_2. Which of the two model specifications (from b) or c)) is preferable? Justify your decision.

2.10.5. Suppose that the two time series x_t and y_t may exhibit seasonal effects. To examine whether there is a significant influence of x_t on y_t, various linear models were estimated. Describe the approach for each model and discuss the associated advantages and disadvantages. In particular, address the risk that t-statistics may be overestimated.

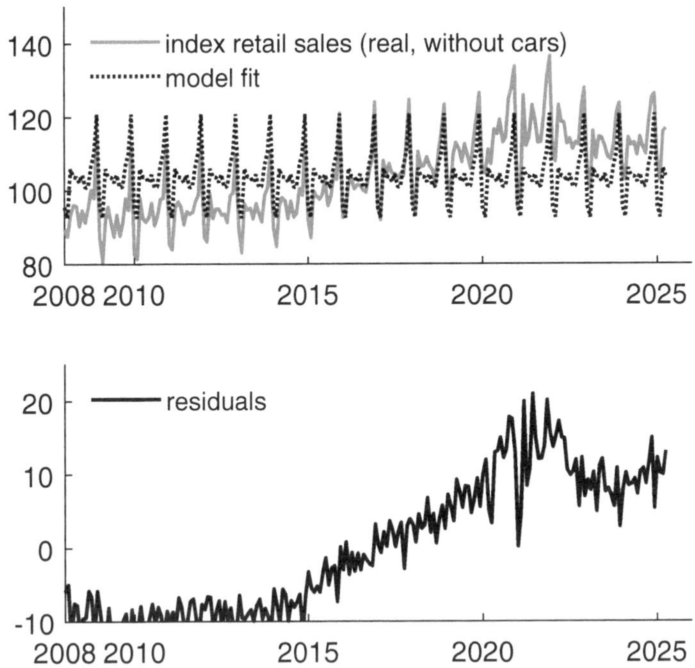

Fig. 2.10 Residuals of model for the index of retail sales with seasonal dummies. (Source: Federal Statistical Office of Germany; GENESIS-Online Database, Table: 45212-0004; own calculations)

(a) Estimation using moving averages of x_t and y_t.
(b) Estimation using the smoothed components derived from the HP filter.
(c) Estimation using seasonal dummies in the regression equation.

2.11 Dynamic Models

2.11.1. Name at least two reasons why dynamic modeling should be considered for economic relationships. What could the practical implementation of a model look like in which only lagged values of the explanatory variables are considered?

2.11.2. Transform an ADL(1,1) model of the form

$$Y_t = \alpha + \alpha_1 Y_{t-1} + \beta_0 X_t + \beta_1 X_{t-1} + \varepsilon_t$$

into its error correction representation.

2.11.3. The following figure shows the result of an ordinary least squares estimation using EViews. The variables denote:

PRIV_CONS: Private consumption in billion euros (in current prices)
DISP_INC: Disposable income in billion euros (in current prices)
@SEAS(k): Seasonal dummy for quarter k
DC_2: A dummy variable for the second quarter 2020 (pandemic)

```
Dep. Variable: D(PRIV_CONS)   Method: Least Squares
Sample: 1991:2 2024:4    Included observations: 135
----------------------------------------------------------
Variable      Coefficient Std. Error   t-Stat.    Prob.
----------------------------------------------------------
C               -0.087468   1.814874   -0.048195  0.9616
@SEAS(1)       -17.65534    1.642591  -10.74847   0.0000
@SEAS(2)        10.59671    2.085619    5.080849  0.0000
@SEAS(3)         5.498079   1.219399    4.508842  0.0000
DC_2           -37.52903    4.571827   -8.208761  0.0000
D(DISP_INC)      0.941826   0.084740   11.11429   0.0000
PRIV_CONS(-1)   -0.333325   0.048606   -6.857728  0.0000
DISP_INC(-1)     0.298203   0.043605    6.838684  0.0000
----------------------------------------------------------
```

(a) What type of econometric model has been analyzed here?
(b) Write out the estimated regression model using standard notation.
(c) Three coefficient estimates from the above regression output are listed again below (rounded). Provide a brief formal interpretation of each estimated parameter.

0.9418:
-0.3333:
0.2982:

(d) What numerical value results from this estimation for the long-run marginal propensity to consume?
(e) Based on the results available from the output above, can you reject the hypothesis that the long-term marginal propensity to consume actually has a numerical value of 0.9?
(f) Suppose that the economy under consideration was in an equilibrium state described by the above regression equation up to time t_0. At t_0, there is a one-time and permanent increase in disposable income. Sketch the course of the dynamic adjustment process of private consumption induced by this increase and discuss your sketch.

2.12 Nonstationarity and Cointegration

2.12.1. Explain the concept of covariance stationarity of a time series.

2.12.2. The following figure provides estimation results of a test equation used to find out whether the variable private consumption in Germany (`PRIV_CONS`) could be considered as covariance stationary. In the software `D(.)` stands for the first difference (Δ) and `.(-1)` etc. denote lagged values (y_{t-1}).

(a) Provide the name of the test used. What is the null hypothesis of this test?

(b) Write down the test equation using the usual notation. You may use y_t for the variable `PRIV_CONS` to ease notation.

(c) Which number provided in the output corresponds to the test statistic?

(d) Is the output provided sufficient to decide whether the null hypothesis must be rejected at the 5% level?

```
Dependent Variable: D(PRIV_CONS) Method: Least Squares
Sample (adjusted): 1993Q1 2025Q1
Included observations: 129 after adjustments
-------------------------------------------------------
Variable            Coeffic.  Std. Err.  t-Stat.  Prob.
-------------------------------------------------------
PRIV_CONS(-1)       0.020261  0.009222   2.1971  0.0299
D(PRIV_CONS(-1)) -0.309467  0.084384  -3.6674  0.0004
D(PRIV_CONS(-2)) -0.142193  0.085090  -1.6711  0.0973
D(PRIV_CONS(-3))  0.063037  0.085395   0.7382  0.4618
D(PRIV_CONS(-4))  0.552190  0.070069   7.8806  0.0000
D(PRIV_CONS(-5)) -0.094829  0.086056  -1.1019  0.2727
D(PRIV_CONS(-6)) -0.267392  0.085582  -3.1244  0.0022
D(PRIV_CONS(-7)) -0.426067  0.084166  -5.0622  0.0000
C                -3.258694  3.201953  -1.0177  0.3109
-------------------------------------------------------
```

2.12.3. What is meant by spurious regression (also called "nonsense estimation") in the context of nonstationary time series?

2.12.4. The following figure shows estimates of a linear model for explaining the number of births `BIRTHS` per year in the German state of Thuringia from 1972 to 2024. A test for unit roots could not reject the null hypothesis of non stationarity neither for the variable `BIRTHS` nor for the explanatory variable `X`.

```
Dependent Variable: BIRTHS        Method: Least Squares
Sample: 1972 2024                 Included observations: 53
-----------------------------------------------------
Variable  Coefficient   Std. Error  t-Statistic  Prob.
C           60967.18     3811.676     15.99485  0.0000
X          -2.813796     0.276948    -10.16002  0.0000
-----------------------------------------------------
R-squared          0.669316   Mean dependent var 22994.23
Log likelihood -530.1455   Hannan-Quinn crit. 20.10955
F-statistic      103.2260   Durbin-Watson stat 0.137076
Prob(F-statistic) 0.0000
-----------------------------------------------------
```

(a) How would you interpret the coefficient estimate for `X`? When assuming that all assumptions for OLS are satisfied, would the estimate be statistically significant different from zero?
(b) Does the output show any indication that the estimated relationships could be a spurious regression?
(c) When rerunning the regression with the changes of both variables, i.e. `D(BIRTHS)` and `D(X)`, the t-statistic for `D(X)` becomes -0.4635. Does this support the assumption that the original estimates above might be the result of a spurious regression?
(d) How would your estimation approach change if you know that `X` is just the diameter of a tree growing in Bavaria 50 years earlier compared to the birth years?

2.12.5. Explain the concept of cointegration for non stationary time series.

2.12.6. Explain the two-step procedure of the Engle-Granger method.

2.12.7. Analyzing the time series for private consumption and disposable income for Germany and the period 1991.1 to 2025.1, you find that both variables are non stationary of type I(1) (i.e. the first differences of the series are stationary). Next, you regress consumption on a constant, disposable income, and seasonal dummies. You run a test for non stationarity on the residuals of this regression such as the ADF test. Using the appropriate critical value, you can reject the null hypothesis at the 5% level. Discuss whether all these findings are in favor of cointegration between the two variables or not.

2.13 Diagnosis and Forecasting

2.13.1. The result of a simulation of a specific economic policy measure fundamentally depends on the underlying model. Figure 2.11 sketches the results of a simulation of an (in both cases identical) exogenous permanent shock starting at time $t_0 = 25$ using two different models.

(a) Describe how, starting from a model specification $Y_t = f(X_t) + \varepsilon_t$, the simulated effects of a shock of size ΔX_{t_0} in t_0 can be calculated.

(b) The interpretation of simulated responses of a model is based on a central assumption. Name and discuss this assumption.

(c) In which aspect do the two models used for the simulation differ?

(d) Suppose your task was to simulate the effects of an expansionary fiscal policy on GDP using an econometric model. Which of the two prototype models outlined above would you prefer for this task? Justify your choice.

(e) Consider the following model, based on which the effects of a one-time permanent positive exogenous shock in period $t = 1$ on the level of the variable y_t have been simulated.

$$\Delta y_t = \beta \Delta x_t - \lambda(y_{t-1} - \alpha x_{t-1}) + \varepsilon_t$$

You can find three different parameter constellations in the table below

Case	β	λ	α
(1)	0	0.15	0.8
(2)	1.6	0.15	0.8
(3)	0.4	0.15	0.8

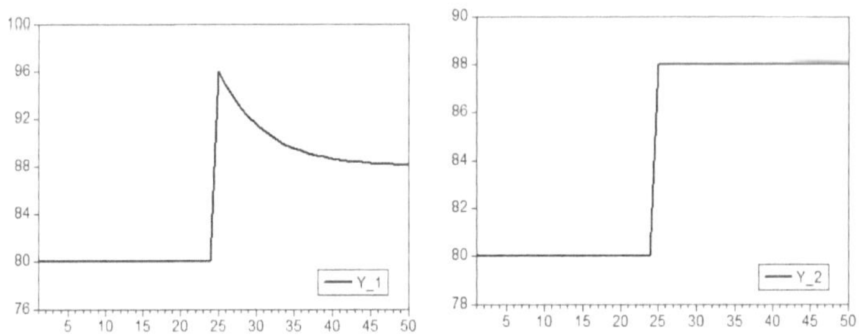

Figure 1) Figure 2)

Fig. 2.11 Simulated responses to a policy shock

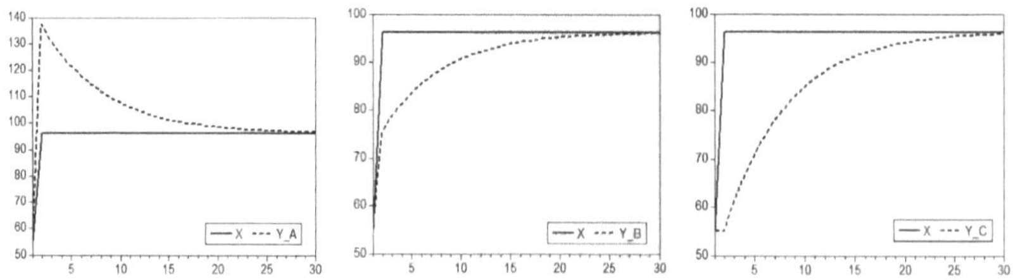

Figure (A) Figure (B) Figure (C)

Fig. 2.12 Simulated responses

Table 2.7 Oil Price Forecast

Month	June	July	Aug.	Sept.	Oct.	Nov.	Dec.	Jan.
Brent	102.47	97.86	93.05	88.91	80.28	73.15	57.67	44.02
Forecast	102.73	96.93	94.25	86.44	78.63	63.87	52.70	48.46

The corresponding adjustment processes are shown graphically in Fig. 2.12 (dotted lines), although possibly in a permuted order.

Assign each of the figures (A)–(C) to one parameter constellation (1)–(3) from the table above and justify your assignment.

2.13.2. A simple, yet widely used model to forecast oil prices is based on so-called futures contracts. These reflect market participants' expectations about the future development of the oil price and are traded on stock exchanges. Table 2.7 shows the oil price (Brent) and the forecasts generated using futures prices for the period from June 2014 to January 2015:

(a) A mean forecast error of 1.675 was calculated for the forecast. What conclusion do you draw from this result?

(b) Furthermore, a root mean squared forecast error (RMSE) of 11.90 was calculated for the forecast. Briefly explain what the RMSE represents and what value it would ideally have for (nearly) perfect forecasts.

(c) The following output shows the result of an ordinary least squares estimation with EViews for the period from April 1994 to January 2015.

```
Dependent Variable: Brent          Method: Least Squares
Sample: 1 17646               Included observations: 250
------------------------------------------------------
Variable   Coefficient  Std. Error  t-Statistic  Prob.
------------------------------------------------------
C           0.089059     0.333888    0.266732   0.7899
Forecast    0.993095     0.005119    193.9837   0.0000
------------------------------------------------------
```

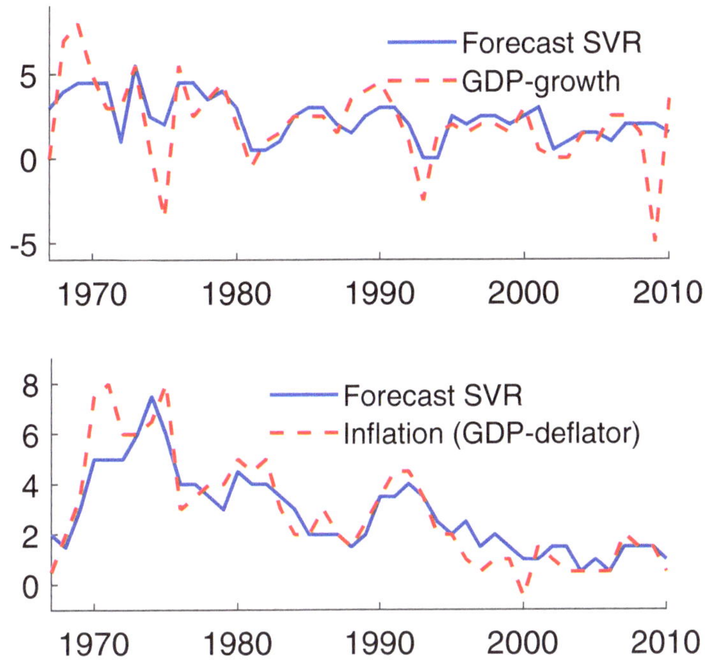

Fig. 2.13 Forecasts for GDP and GDP deflator. (Source: Data from Heilemann and Stekler (2012), German Economic Review, 14(2), p. 240, "Has the Accuracy of Macroeconomic Forecasts for Germany Improved? Own illustration")

Interpret the coefficients. Is there a systematic bias in the futures model forecast?

(d) Propose a suitable "naive" forecast for the oil price that could be used to compare the forecast based on futures contracts. Briefly justify your choice.

2.13.3. Figure 2.13 shows the forecasts of the German Council of Economic Experts (Sachverständigenrat zur Begutachtung der gesamtwirtschaftlichen Entwicklung, SVR) as gray lines and the actual realizations (dashed lines) for the growth rates of real GDP (top) and the GDP deflator (bottom) in Germany for the years 1967 to 2010.

(a) For the SVR forecasts of real GDP growth, a Root Mean Squared Error (RMSE) of 1.9218 was calculated. Please briefly explain what is measured by the RMSE and what value it would ideally assume for (almost) perfect forecasts.

(b) Two alternative forecasts were considered. The first one assumes a constant growth rate of zero for GDP, while for the second it was assumed that current GDP growth would be equal to previous year's growth. For the first approach, the RMSE value was 2.7313, and for the second 1.3956. Based on these results, what conclusion can be drawn about the quality of the SVR forecasts in the observed period? In your reasoning, please also address the concept of Theil's U.

(c) Propose a suitable "naive" forecast for the growth rate of the GDP deflator, with which the corresponding SVR forecast could be compared. Briefly justify your choice.

2.13.4. To forecast the development of the German industrial production index, the ZEW Economic Sentiment Indicator based on a survey of financial market experts about their economic expectations for six months ahead and the truck toll performance index published by the Federal Statistical Office are used.

(a) Briefly explain which type of indicators these are (in terms of their temporal relation to the industrial production index). Based on your classification, a model based on Which index is more likely to derive a good forecast of industrial production?

(b) To measure the relationship between `IP` (industrial production index) and `ZEWSENT` (ZEW sentiment indicator, which can take values between −100 and +100), a linear regression model was estimated, where `IPGR6` denotes the growth rate in industrial production compared to six months before ($\texttt{IPGR} = \ln \texttt{IP}_t - \ln \texttt{IP}_{t-6}$). The output of the estimation is:

```
Dependent Variable: IPGR6            Method: Least Squares
Sample: 1992:6 2025:1           Included observations: 392
-------------------------------------------------------
Variable    Coefficient  Std. Error  t-Statistic  Prob.
-------------------------------------------------------
C              -0.780360    0.261213   -2.987445   0.0030
ZEWSENT(-6)  0.051108    0.006075    8.412218   0.0000
-------------------------------------------------------
R-squared              0.15358  Mean dependent var 0.29589
Adjusted R-squared 0.15141  S.D. dependent var 4.89472
F-statistic            70.7654  Durbin-Watson stat 0.53037
-------------------------------------------------------
```

- Please interpret the regression results shown. Also discuss the economic relevance of the results.
- Since this is a time series regression, there is generally a risk of bias due to autocorrelated error terms. Based on the reported results, does this problem appear in the current estimation?

(c) The change in the truck toll performance index shows a significantly positive relationship with the change in industrial production. In your opinion, is it also fundamentally suitable for a forecast horizon of 6 months? Please briefly explain your assessment.

3 Text-Related Exercises

All exercises in this chapter are based on short texts dealing with empirical economics or econometric methods. Therefore, before starting to think about possible answers to the questions, you should read the texts indicated. This provides a chance to examine real examples of empirical economic research. The discussion provided on some of the questions in Chap. 6 should be taken as suggestions rather than as comprehensive and conclusive answers, since the evaluation of empirical research does not always provide a clear, simple correct answer.

3.1 Tasks and Principles of Empirical Economic Research

3.1.1 The following questions are based on the first chapter of the annual report 2024/2025 of the German Council of Economic Experts, which you can find in https://www.sachverstaendigenrat-wirtschaft.de/fileadmin/dateiablage/gutachten/jg202425/JG202425_Chapter_1.pdf. For answering the questions, it might be sufficient reading the brief summary on pages 2–5.

(a) Central tasks of empirical economic research are the analysis of past developments, e.g., to assess the quality of economic models or the quantification of relationships, the evaluation of the current situation (diagnosis) and the (conditional) forecast of future developments. What role do these tasks play in the indicated chapter of the report? Provide an example in the text for each relevant task.

(b) Explain the concept of a conditional forecast and provide examples from the text for conditions underlying the economic outlook shown in Chart 1 of the chapter.

P. Winker et al., *Exercise Book Empirical Economic Research and Econometrics*, https://doi.org/10.1007/978-3-662-72713-3_3

3.1.2 In their paper on "Active pension mainly relieves higher-earning pensioners; employment effects are uncertain" published in the DIW Weekly Report 25/26/2025, pp. 143–149 (https://doi.org/10.18723/diw_dwr:2025-25-1), Bach, Buslei, Geyer, and Haan (2025) discuss the possible impact of tax benefits for older employees. Please read the paper before responding to the following questions.

(a) Which of the central tasks of empirical economic research is addressed by the empirical analysis presented in the paper? Why is this contribution relevant for the political decision whether to introduce the suggested change or not?

(b) The authors also discuss whether tax benefits should also be introduced for self-employed persons or not. Can this question be answered solely on the basis of the available information from their study?

3.2 Data Basis of Empirical Economic Research

3.2.1 Jansen, Wang, Paul, and Hoekstra published 2024 a review paper on the discussion on "Beyond GDP" (https://www.thelancet.com/pdfs/journals/lanplh/PIIS2542-5196(24)00147-5.pdf). Based on your reading, you might answer the following questions:

(a) List at least two aspects with are considered sub-optimal when using GDP as a measure of overall welfare.

(b) What is the conceptional approach proposed in the paper for an improved concept taking into account also aspects of inclusion and sustainability?

(c) What suggestions do the authors make with regard to the measurement of broader concepts of well-being?

3.2.2 Read the methodological notes on foreign direct investment provided by Deutsche Bundesbank (2019) (https://www.bundesbank.de/resource/blob/798350/272c026ee4986284fc8e72e8b224befd/472B63F073F071307366337C94F8C870/methodische-erlaeuterungen-direktinvestitionen-data.pdf). Then answer the following questions.

(a) For which sets of statistics is the measurement of foreign direct investment (FDI) relevant? Why does it seem adequate to use a benchmark definition for all OECD countries?

(b) Describe the concept of FDI measurement by the Deutsche Bundesbank and its operationalization. Does the threshold value of 10% appear sensible in this context?

(c) With regard to longer chains of ownership, the paper mentions a difference between the methodology used by the Deutsche Bundesbank and the international benchmark. What exactly is this difference? Would German FDI abroad become larger or smaller when the benchmark definition would be applied one-to-one.

3.3 Data Processing

3.3.1 In Working Paper 2773 of the European Central Bank, Menz, Wieland, and Beck (2023, revised 2025) analyze the impact of quality adjustment on consumer price inflation (https://www.ecb.europa.eu/pub/pdf/scpwps/ecb.wp2773~6e0b9467b4.sv.pdf?4a61209faa58ed0c1590bc1da8f526b2). For answering the following questions, you might concentrate on reading Section 3 of the paper.

(a) Describe the idea of alternative methods for adjusting prices for changes in the quality of products.

(b) Describe in more detail the method actually used for the present study.

(c) List at least one product for which quality adjustment increases actual inflation rates and one for which the inflation rate is decreased by quality adjustment. Please explain also the reason for the different impact of quality adjustment for the two products.

(d) How large is the overall impact of quality adjustments on consumer price inflation for the years 2010–2020 estimated by the authors? Why do they consider their estimate to be a lower bound of the actual values?

3.4 Economic Indicators

3.4.1 The occasional paper No. 265 for the European Central Bank (ECB), published in September 2021, discusses "Inflation measurement and its assessment in the ECB's monetary policy strategy review" (https://www.ecb.europa.eu/pub/pdf/scpops/ecb.op265~a3fb0b611d.en.pdf). Before answering the following questions, you should read at least the first four chapters of this paper.

(a) First, you should explain the ECB's price stability concept, which should include both the quantitative goal and the arguments for using the harmonized consumer price index (HICP) for this purpose in the first place.

(b) What adjustments have been made in the calculation of the HCIP since 2023 and for what purpose?

(c) Which sources of potential measurement bias and uncertainty are discussed in Chap. 3 of the paper?

(d) Why is the inclusion of the cost of owner-occupied housing (OOH) considered crucial by the authors of the article? What are the advantages or disadvantages of different approaches to this end?

3.4.2 Read the section "The global disinflation process and its costs" (pp. 18–21) in the Monthly Report for July 2024 from the Deutsche Bundesbank. https://publikationen.bundesbank.de/publikationen-en/reports-studies/monthly-reports/monthly-report-july-2024-935476?article=the-global-disinflation-process-and-its-costs-935482

(a) Explain in your own words how the consumer price index (CPI) evolved in the leading industrial economies since early 2021. What historical peak levels, comparable to the 1980s, were reached?
(b) Describe at least three factors identified in the text as drivers of the post-pandemic inflation surge.
(c) Describe the role of demand shocks (especially shifts in consumption behavior) and supply bottlenecks.
(d) Explain how the combination of higher demand for goods and constrained supply affected production costs.
(e) What additional impact did Russia's war against Ukraine have on global inflation, especially in terms of food and energy?

3.4.3 There exist different concepts for measuring poverty. One distinction is between absolute and relative poverty. Absolute poverty implies that humans do not have access to what is necessary for survival. In contrast, relative poverty is often defined by reference to some quantiles or means of the income distribution in a specific region.

Please read the executive summary of the The Federal Government's Sixth Report on Poverty and Wealth (https://www.armuts-und-reichtumsbericht.de/SharedDocs/Downloads/Berichte/sixth-report-on-poverty-and-wealth.pdf?__blob=publicationFile&v=2) published in 2021. In particular, pages 13 to 17 are relevant to answer the following questions.

(a) Is the concept of the "at-risk-of-poverty rate" based on an absolute or relative concept of poverty?
(b) How would the "at-risk-of-poverty rate" change if all incomes considered for the analysis would increase by a factor of two?
(c) What type of concept is underlying the "(severe) material deprivation rate"? How would this ratio tend to change if all incomes considered were doubled?

3.5 Input-Output Analysis

3.5.1 Read Sections 2.1 and 2.2 of the paper "Gross Employment Effects in the Renewable Energy Industry in Germany: An Input-Output Analysis from 2000 to 2018" by O'Sullivan and Edler (2024) in Sustainability 2020, 12, 6163, which can be found at https://www.mdpi.com/2071-1050/12/15/6163/pdf?version=1596158615. Then, you may answer the following questions:

(a) The authors want to study the employment effect of the renewable energy industry in Germany. What do they consider to be the main advantage of using input-output analysis in this context?
(b) What drawback do the authors see regarding the Germany input-output table with 71 production sectors? How do they try to overcome this shortcoming?
(c) The employment effects are derived from the extended input-output table by means of the so-called "labor coefficients". Explain whether these coefficients rather follow the concept of input or output coefficients for input-output tables.

3.5.2 Before addressing the following questions, you should read Box 3 on pages 46ff in the Economic Bulletin 1/2022 of the European Central Bank (https://www.ecb.europa.eu/pub/pdf/ecbu/eb202201.en.pdf).
(a) The authors claim that "supply chain linkages amplify the reaction of goods producers and services providers to gas price increases". Provide an explicit example of such supply chain linkages related to one of the industries shown in Chart B on page 48.
(b) Chart C shows the impact of a hypothetical 10% gas rationing shock. Explain the difference between direct and indirect effects. How is the shock introduced in an input-output model?

3.6 The Econometric Model

3.6.1 Read the article by William H. White (1969): "How Useful Are Econometric Models?", Finance & Development, 6 (1), 23–29 (http://doi.org/10.5089/9781616352936.022.A004). Then, try to answer the following questions:
(a) What is the major difference between a model from physics and an econometric model according to the author?
(b) Describe the origin of the gaps between any econometric model and the actual data.
(c) Why is an econometric model better suited to study the relationship between variables in more complex settings than a simple cause-and-effect relationship, as discussed in the paragraph headed "Discovering the Model Without Benefit of Laboratory Experiment?"
(d) Which potential applications of econometric models are discussed in the article (mainly on page 25)?

3.7 The Linear Regression Model

3.7.1 In his article "Oil production responses to price changes: an empirical application of the competitive model to OPEC and non-OPEC countries" (Energy Economics

24, 2002, p. 97–106) (https://doi.org/10.1016/S0140-9883(01)00091-3), the author analyzes oil production in the major oil producing countries. For the period 1973–1997, he estimates regression models of the type (see equation (1) on page 101):

$$lnQ_t = \alpha + \gamma lnP_t + \beta t + \varepsilon_t \,,$$

where the following notation is used:

lnQ : natural logarithm of oil production quantity (1000 barrels/day)
lnP : natural logarithm of real price of crude oil (US-$/barrel)
t : time index

(a) Explain the estimation approach: How can the specification be theoretically justified? What role does the parameter γ play here?
(b) The results of estimation (based on yearly observations) are summarized in Table 2 on page 102. First, consider the estimated results for the OPEC aggregate and record them in equation form. Based on this equation, what behavior would you expect for the OPEC aggregate if the real price of crude oil increased by 1%?
(c) For comparison, note the estimated regression equation for the non-OPEC aggregate. What response does this equation predict for an increase 1% in the real price of crude oil?
(d) What is the author's economic interpretation for the qualitatively different results addressed in questions (b) and (c)?
(e) Do you agree with this interpretation or do you see methodological reservations? Explain your assessment.

3.9 Qualitative Variable

3.9.1 In the DIW Weekly Report 16+17/2025 (https://www.diw.de/de/diw_01.c.947085.de/publikationen/weekly_reports/2025_16/heft.html), Kerstin Bernoth analyzes the European Central Bank's (ECB) interest rate decisions using a multinomial ordered probit model (essentially an extension of the probit model). The dependent variable is qualitative with three categories: rate decrease (− 1), no change (0), and rate increase (+ 1). This model assumes that the observed categorical change in the key interest rate is based on a latent, continuous variable influenced by various explanatory factors. To answer the following questions, please refer to Box 2 on page 104 of the report, which outlines the model specification, estimated coefficients, and the methodology used for forecasting.

(a) Explain why an ordered probit model is more appropriate for modeling this three-category qualitative dependent variable than a linear regression model.

Provide at least two reasons why linear regression might be less well suited in this setting.

(b) The model uses two threshold parameters (τ_1 and τ_2) to separate the categories of the dependent variable. Describe the role of these thresholds in the model and how they affect the probabilities of each interest rate decision.

(c) The latent variable Δi_t^* is modeled as a linear function of explanatory variables X_t, including the ECB Communication Stance Indicator (CI). Explain how a positive estimated coefficient β for CI affects the probabilities of the three possible outcomes of the qualitative indicator for the interest rate.

(d) Briefly describe how a "one-step ahead" forecast is conducted with this model. Why are the explanatory variables shifted one period into the past in this approach?

(e) How could you examine whether the variable "geopolitical risks" plays an important role in explaining ECB interest rate decisions? Describe how you would proceed and how you could judge the statistical significance and economic relevance of the variable based on the estimation output.

3.10 Trend and Seasonal Adjustment

3.10.1 Read the text in Box 5 on pages 47–50 of the Monthly Bulletin October 2007 of the European Central Bank (ECB) (http://www.ecb.europa.eu/pub/pdf/mobu/mb200710en.pdf) before answering the following questions:

(a) What role do measures of capacity utilization measures play in the context of European monetary policy?

(b) What role do capacity utilization figures play in business cycle analysis? In your explanation, please also discuss the type of business cycle indicators they represent.

(c) Describe the capacity utilization rate survey conducted by the European Commission's industry and consumer survey. What variable is to be determined in this survey?

(d) Why are deviations from the 'trend' shown in Figure C (p. 49)?

3.10.2 Read the Box on "he impact of weather conditions on gross domestic product in the latter part of 2013 and early part of 2014" on pages 54–55 of the Monthly Report of the Deutsche Bundesbank for May 2014 (https://www.bundesbank.de/resource/blob/707430/8b27a29a56996fadccb0161fd21be35b/472B63F073F071307366337C94F8C870/2014-05-economic-conditions-germany-data.pdf). Then, answer the following questions:

(a) What is the difference between seasonal and weather effects? Are weather effects also taken into account in seasonal adjustment?

(b) Describe the procedure proposed by the Bundesbank for weather adjustment as specifically as possible (preferably with the aid of a formal model representation). What could be meant by the term 'residual weather effects' mentioned in the article?

(c) Why could higher growth in the first quarter of 2014 due to weather conditions lead to lower growth rates in the following quarters? Is this to be expected for 2014?

3.10.3 The April 2013 monthly report from Deutsche Bundesbank (https://www.bundesbank.de/en/publications/reports/monthly-reports/monthly-report-april-2013-670522) contains an insert on pages 31–35 on the topic 'Determining aggregate trend output in the USA'. Please read these pages and then answer the following questions:

(a) The article describes two methods for determining the trend component of a time series. Briefly outline the procedure for both methods.

(b) In the figure on top of page 32, the challenge of selecting the appropriate reference period is illustrated for one of the methods. Describe the influence that the selection of the reference period can have on the estimated trend component. How strong is this effect in the specific example?

(c) The figure on top of page 33 illustrates the so-called endpoint problem that can arise when using the second method. Explain this issue in your own words. How relevant are the effects on the measurement of the trend output in 2007? What method is proposed in the text to reduce the extent of the problem?

(d) When determining the current state of an economy, other relevant issues mentioned in the text are data availability and revisions. Briefly describe both problems using GDP as an example.

3.11 Dynamic Models

3.11.1 The following questions should be answered after having read the box on "Interest rate pass- through into bank loans and customer deposits" on pages 49–51 of the monthly report June 2023 of the Deutsche Bundesbank (https://www.bundesbank.de/resource/blob/912874/bc2a808c9fd5f9611eec77b2d061a8ee/472B63F073F071307366337C94F8C870/2023-06-zinsentwicklung-data.pdf).

(a) Explain why the error correction models are considered by the authors as well-suited for modeling the reaction of bank lending and deposit rates to changes in market rates.

(b) Write down the estimated model using r_t^M as symbol for the market rate and r_t^B for the bank rate used. Indicate which parameters in your model correspond to the columns in the tables on pages 50 and 51 labeled *Immediate pass-through*, *Adjustment speed*, and *Long-term pass-through*. You can ignore the rows with results for the Euro area.

(c) Do the estimated coefficients correspond to your expectations? What differences in dynamic adjustment can be observed between lending and deposit rates, respectively. How are these differences explained?

3.12 Nonstationarity and Cointegration

3.12.1 Read the paper "A regression-based approach to the CO_2 airborne fraction" by M. Bennedsen, E. Hillebrand, and S.J. Koopman, Nature Communications 2024 (https://doi.org/10.1038/s41467-024-52728-1). You can focus on the first two subsections of Results (pp. 2–3). After reading, answer the following questions:

(a) Explain the idea of the Dickey-Fuller test applied to the two time series G_t and E_t. What are the findings with respect to the (non)stationarity of these series?

(b) What risk would result from estimating the simple linear regression model $G_t = \alpha E_t + u_t$ and interpreting the t-statistic for the estimated coefficient $\hat{\alpha}$?

(c) The authors argue that estimating the model is fine based on a test they run in addition on the residuals $\hat{u}_t$. Explain the idea of this test, its name, and the result. Would you agree with the authors that running the regression is a sensible approach in this setting?

(d) The authors also ran a Jarque-Bera test for the residuals. What is the null hypothesis of this test? Does the null hypothesis have to be rejected? What are the consequences of the finding?

3.13 Diagnosis and Forecasting

3.13.1 Read Box 1.1 of the World Economic Outlook 2023 published by the International Monetary Fund (https://www.imf.org/en/Publications/WEO/Issues/2023/10/10/world-economic-outlook-october-2023) on the medium-term GDP growth projections and answer the following questions.

(a) Based on the text, explain the role of trend components in forecasting medium-term growth. How do forecasters use trend adjustments to correct for biases?

(b) Identify the main sources of change in per capita output growth mentioned in the text. How could these factors affect the trend component of the economic data?

3.13.2 Read Section 3: "Measurement of Inflation Expectations" (pp. 12–15) of the paper "Inflation expectations: models and measures" provided by Alcidi, Gros and Shamsfakhr (2022) for the European Parliament's Committee on Economic and Monetary Affairs (ECON) (http://www.europarl.europa.eu/RegData/etudes/IDAN/2022/703338/IPOL_IDA(2022)703338_EN.pdf).

(a) Identify and describe the two main broad categories of measures of inflation expectations discussed in this section. For each category, explain the fundamental principle behind its measurement.
(b) Discuss the advantages and disadvantages of using survey-based measures of inflation expectations, as presented in the paper. Provide specific examples of the survey-based measures mentioned and explain what insights they offer.
(c) Explain the concept of market-based measures of inflation expectations. How are these measures derived and what are their main benefits and limitations compared to survey-based measures? Give examples of market-based indicators discussed in the text.
(d) Compare and contrast the information provided by short-term versus long-term inflation expectations, as discussed in this section. Why is it important for central banks to monitor both and what different policy implications might each horizon suggest?

Part II

Solutions

4 Solutions for Multiple Choice Questions

In this chapter, you will find all sample solutions to the multiple-choice, true or false, and completion questions. Some solutions are accompanied by brief additional explanations. The sample solutions are intended to help you assess your own performance. You should try to solve the exercises independently or with the help of a textbook before consulting the sample solutions. The numbering of the solutions corresponds to the numbering of the questions.

4.1 Tasks and Principles of Empirical Economic Research

1.1.1 (b)
1.1.2 (b)
1.1.3 (c)
1.1.4 (d)
1.1.5 (d)
1.1.6 (a)
1.1.7 (d)
1.1.8 (c)

4.2 Data Basis of Empirical Economic Research

1.2.1 (d)
1.2.2 (a)
1.2.3 (b)
1.2.4 validity; objectivity; panel

P. Winker et al., *Exercise Book Empirical Economic Research and Econometrics*,
https://doi.org/10.1007/978-3-662-72713-3_4

1.2.5 true
1.2.6 false
1.2.7 true
1.2.8 true
1.2.9 uncertainty principle; revision
1.2.10 (c)
1.2.11 (a)
1.2.12 false
1.2.13 (d)—While solution option (a) sounds very similar, it only refers to the respondents. Since a significant share of respondents usually do not answer, the distribution of age and sex in the sample will still differ from that of the population.
1.2.14 False, because it cannot be assumed that all selected individuals will respond, and this "non-response" may not be random. It could depend on the variables relevant to the study.
1.2.15 (b)—Solution option (d) is incorrect because representativeness is not about the size of the sample. As long as the sample does not fully cover the population, there is a risk of a selective sample and therefore of lack of representativeness. However, in practice, this problem occurs less frequently with larger samples.
1.2.16 (c) For the specific context of decision making, leading indicators are especially needed, making D the first choice. Clearly, A and B have little informational value and E has none at all.

4.3 Data Processing

1.3.1 (c)
1.3.2 (linear) interpolation; extrapolation; elasticity
1.3.3 (c)
1.3.4 (d)
1.3.5 False. However, this additivity holds when using logarithmic growth rates $\Delta ln(x) = ln(x_t) - ln(x_{t-1})$.
1.3.6 True
1.3.7 Laspeyres; Paasche
1.3.8 (d)
1.3.9 True
1.3.10 False, because there are also so-called "improper ratios". This is the case, for example, with exports, which by definition are not a subset of GDP (this only applies to the trade surplus, i.e. exports minus imports). The government debt ratio is also an "unreal ratio" as it relates a stock variable (government debt) to a flow variable (GDP), which means that ratios greater than 1 (that is, over 100%) can be observed for many countries.

4.4 Economic Indicators

1.4.1 Plausibility; Conformity
1.4.2 (c)
1.4.3 (c)
1.4.4 (a)
1.4.5 (c)
1.4.6 (a)
1.4.7 (b)
1.4.8 False
1.4.9 (a)
1.4.10 core inflation; reporting rate; persons leaving unemployment
1.4.11 (d)
1.4.12 True
1.4.13 (d)
1.4.14 (b) The slope of all Lorenz curves does not decrease, which is the case of A (at the value of 0.3) and E (throughout).
1.4.15 (d)
1.4.16 (b)
1.4.17 False
1.4.18 wage share; Lorenz curve
1.4.19 (c)
1.4.20 (b)
1.4.21 (b)
1.4.22 False

4.5 Input-Output Analysis

1.5.1 (d)
1.5.2 output coefficient; input coefficient
1.5.3 True
1.5.4 (a)
1.5.5 (b)
1.5.6 (c)
1.5.7 True

4.6 The Econometric Model

1.6.1 (c)
1.6.2 (b)
1.6.3 (d)
1.6.4 False
1.6.5 (d)
1.6.6 (a)
1.6.7 (b)

4.7 The Linear Regression Model

1.7.1 False, because for the linear model we obtain:

$$\min_{\hat{\beta}} \sum_{t=1}^{T} \hat{\varepsilon}_t{}^2 = \sum_{t=1}^{T} (Y_t - \hat{\beta})^2$$

$$\Leftrightarrow \frac{\partial (\sum_{t=1}^{T} (Y_t - \hat{\beta})^2}{\partial \hat{\beta}} = -2\sum_{t=1}^{T} (Y_t - \hat{\beta}) = 0$$

$$\Leftrightarrow \hat{\beta} = \frac{1}{T}\sum_{t=1}^{T} Y_t = \overline{Y}$$

1.7.2 unbiased; efficient
1.7.3 (d)
1.7.4 True
1.7.5 (d) The coefficient of determination is defined as:

$$R^2 = 1 - \frac{\sum_{i=1}^{n}(Y_i - \hat{Y}_i)^2}{\sum_{i=1}^{n}(Y_i - \overline{Y})^2}$$

R^2 is exactly zero when the numerator and the denominator are equal. In this case, the line has no slope ($\beta_2 = 0$). Thus, there is no linear relationship.

1.7.6 (a)
1.7.7 True
1.7.8 (c)

1.7.9 False
1.7.10 (b)
1.7.11 (b)
1.7.12 False. The t-statistic under the null hypothesis can be calculated as follows:

$$t = \frac{\hat{\beta}_i - 1}{\sqrt{\widehat{V(\hat{\beta}_i)}}} = \frac{0.978 - 1}{0.0075} = -2.9333$$

At a significance level of $\alpha = 0.05$, this results in a rejection region

$$[-\infty, -1.96] \wedge [1.96, +\infty].$$

Since $t \in [-\infty, -1.96]$, we can reject the null hypothesis.

1.7.13 True. The t-statistic under the null hypothesis can be calculated as follows:

$$t = \frac{\hat{\beta}_i - 1}{\sqrt{\widehat{V(\hat{\beta}_i)}}} = \frac{0.07 - 0.1}{0.025} = -1.2$$

At a significance level of $\alpha = 0.05$, the rejection region is given by

$$[-\infty, -1.96] \wedge [1.96, +\infty].$$

Since $t \notin [-\infty, -1.96]$, we **cannot** reject the null hypothesis.

1.7.14 (c)
1.7.15 (a)
1.7.16 (c)
1.7.17 coefficient of determination/R^2, F
1.7.18 (a) The R^2 values of the simulated examples are 0.0645 (A), 0.9235 (B), 0.5305 (C), and 0.0006 (D).

4.8 Residual Analysis and Check of Model Assumptions

1.8.1 (c)
1.8.2 True
1.8.3 False, because higher-order autocorrelation or nonlinear dependencies are also possible.
1.8.4 False. This is an indication of the heteroskedasticity of the error terms.
1.8.5 Durbin-Watson test; White; Breusch-Godfrey
1.8.6 (d)
1.8.7 (b)
1.8.8 (d)

4.9 Qualitative Variables

1.9.1 (a)

1.9.2 (c) In this example, the X matrix would look as follows:

$$\mathbf{X} = \begin{pmatrix} 1 \ 1 \ 0 \ \text{AGE}_1 \ \text{GIESSEN}_1 \\ 1 \ 0 \ 1 \ \text{AGE}_2 \ \text{GIESSEN}_2 \\ \vdots \ \vdots \ \vdots \quad \vdots \qquad \vdots \\ 1 \ 0 \ 1 \ \text{AGE}_i \ \text{GIESSEN}_i \end{pmatrix}.$$

This matrix does not have full column rank, as the first three columns are not linearly independent. The first column can always be written as the sum of the second and third columns. Therefore, $(X'X)^{-1}$ does not exist and the coefficients cannot be uniquely determined.

1.9.3 True

1.9.4 (d)

1.9.5 (c)

1.9.6 True. In the linear probability model, the coefficients can be interpreted as partial derivatives of the probabilities with respect to the explanatory variables.

1.9.7 (c)

1.9.8 (d)

1.9.9 (b)

1.9.10 (b)—If this were a linear probability model for which the coefficient estimates are provided in the table, one could calculate the effect of a 1% increase in income: `ln(Income)` would then increase by 0.01, and the probability by $0.01 \cdot 0.095$.

1.9.11 (c)

4.10 Trend and Seasonal Adjustment

1.10.1 (d) The magnitude of the weekly fluctuations (lower values on weekends) apparently depends on the level of the series.

1.10.2 True

1.10.3 (b)

1.10.4 (c)

1.10.5 endpoint problem; Berlin/BV4.1

1.10.6 (c)

1.10.7 (d)

1.10.8 (a)

4.11 Dynamic Models

1.11.1 (c)

1.11.2 (c) The general form of the error correction model can be represented and rearranged as follows:

$$\begin{aligned}\Delta(\texttt{GASOLINE})_t &= \beta_0 + \beta_1 \Delta(\texttt{OIL})_t - \gamma(\texttt{GASOLINE}_{t-1} - \alpha_1 \texttt{OIL}_{t-1}) + \varepsilon_t \\ &= \beta_0 + \beta_1 \Delta(\texttt{OIL})_t - \gamma \texttt{GASOLINE}_{t-1} + \gamma\alpha_1 \texttt{OIL}_{t-1} + \varepsilon_t \\ &= \beta_0 + \beta_1 \Delta(\texttt{OIL})_t + \beta_2 \texttt{GASOLINE}_{t-1} + \beta_3 \texttt{OIL}_{t-1} + \varepsilon_t\end{aligned}$$

The error correction model implies that the estimator β_2 must have a negative sign. The estimator for the parameter of the long-term equilibrium must be calculated from the estimators. Therefore:

$$\hat{\alpha_1} = \frac{\hat{\beta_3}}{-\hat{\beta_2}} = \frac{0.007}{-(-0.25)} = 0.028$$

1.11.3 information; 6; error correction model

1.11.4 (a)

4.12 Non-Stationarity and Cointegration

1.12.1 (c)

1.12.2 True

1.12.3 False

1.12.4 (a)

1.12.5 (covariance) stationarity; ADF; cointegration relationship

1.12.6 (a)

1.12.7 error correction model; representation theorem; spurious correlation

1.12.8 False

4.13 Diagnostics and Forecasting

1.13.1 (c)

1.13.2 (a)

1.13.3 False

1.13.4 Theil's inequality coefficient (Theil's U); evaluation; Diebold-Mariano

1.13.5 (b)

1.13.6 True

1.13.7 (a)

Solutions for Selected Exercises 5

In this chapter, you will find some solutions or hints for some selected exercises presented in Chap. 2. Please note that many questions may not have a single correct answer, e.g., when examples are requested. The sample solutions are intended to help you check your own performance. You should therefore try to solve the questions independently first before consulting the sample solutions. The numbering of the solutions corresponds to the numbering of the questions.

5.1 Tasks and Principles of Empirical Economic Research

2.1.1 Within the framework of the deductive-inductive approach in economic research, the following typical steps can be described: First, a **theory** is derived from the observation of real phenomena through **abstraction**. In this context, the term "theory" is used in a broad sense and is not limited to mathematically formal models. In theory development, it is important to capture the essential aspects of the relationship under consideration without obscuring them with too many details. Through **logical deductions** within the theoretical model, **conclusions** can be drawn, which are then brought back from the abstract level of the model to **implications for real phenomena** using **interpretation**. These implications may, for example, refer to transmission channels, multiplier effects, or elasticities. Econometric methods (in the narrow sense) then serve the purpose of **evaluating** these conclusions, that is, clarifying whether the conclusions and the real phenomena are consistent with each other or not. If the conclusions and observed real-world phenomena are consistent, the derived model cannot be rejected, at least.

P. Winker et al., *Exercise Book Empirical Economic Research and Econometrics*,
https://doi.org/10.1007/978-3-662-72713-3_5

This explanation makes it clear that within the framework of an econometric analysis (in the broader sense), a close interaction between economic modeling, real phenomena (which are reflected in data) and suitable statistical methods is always necessary.

2.1.2 No sample solution.

2.1.3 No sample solution.
Hint: It is crucial to recognize that income inequality, in addition to a potential impact on economic growth, also has a number of further implications. For example, questions of equal opportunities or the ethical acceptability of very low incomes are raised. These questions cannot be answered by empirical economic research alone.

5.2 Data Basis of Empirical Economic Research

2.2.1 (a) Let C_t denote the number of newly registered infections on day t. Then the equation for a linear trend is given by $C_t = \alpha_0 + \alpha_1 t$, where α_1 represents the daily change in C_t. You can calculate the value α_1 directly by dividing the total increase of 23,399 – 2,503 = 20,896 by the number of days between the two observations (37). This results in $\alpha_1 = 564.76$. Starting from the value on November 7, 2020, the forecast for December 24, 2020, is obtained by adding the daily increase (564.76) multiplied by the number of days from November 7 to December 24 (47) to the initial value of 23,399. This yields a forecast of 49,943 (rounded to a whole number), whereas the actual value was 32,195. Using the same calculation for Easter, which is 148 days after November 7, 2020, results in a a value of 106,983 (actual value: 9,677).
Alternatively, the parameters α_0 and α_1 can be obtained as the solution of the following linear system of equations (assuming that October 1, 2020, is day 275 and November 7, 2020, is day 312 of the year):

$$2{,}503 = \alpha_0 + \alpha_1 \cdot 275$$

$$23{,}399 = \alpha_0 + \alpha_1 \cdot 312$$

The values for Christmas Eve and Easter are then obtained by inserting $t = 359$ and $t = 460$, respectively (counting from January 1, 2020).

(b) An exponential trend would be described by $C_t = \beta_0 e^{\beta_1 t}$. Taking the natural logarithm gives $\ln(C_t) = \ln(\beta_0) + \beta_1 t$. The subsequent steps follow exactly those of the linear trend, and using one of the two methods shown, we obtain a value of $\beta_1 = 0.0603$, corresponding to a daily increase of 6.03%. Starting from the value $\ln(23{,}399)$ on November 7, 2020, the forecast for the logarithmic value on December 24, 2020, is $\ln(23{,}399) + 0.0603 \cdot 47 = 12.8945$. Thus,

$e^{12.8945}$ is the forecast for the actual value, which exceeds 398,000. Using the same method for Easter yields a number close to 176 million.

(c) At least in the second case shown in (b), it becomes evident that a purely mechanical projection (extrapolation) of trends is not necessarily plausible. A number of 176 million newly confirmed infections in Germany with about 83 million inhabitants on a single day is mathematically clearly not feasible. Although the assumption of exponential growth may describe the pandemic's short-term dynamics reasonably well, it fails to consider other factors that become significant in the medium to long term. In this particular case, such factors include behavioral changes in the population and political measures in response to rising infection rates, as well as—at very high cumulative infection rates—the increasing immunity of individuals who have already been infected. To account for such factors, simple extrapolation is not sufficient.

2.2.2 To derive concrete data from the real-world phenomena to be described, it is important to examine the individual steps involved in the process from the real phenomenon to concrete numbers, i.e., in particular the theoretical concept, the measurable attributes, the measurement, and the data processing. Each of these steps must be evaluated with respect to validity, reliability, and objectivity.

Using the example of the unemployment rate, it becomes clear that there are alternative approaches, which can indeed lead to different measurement outcomes. These approaches differ not only in their measurement methods, but already in the operationalization of the concept of unemployment.

In Table 5.1, we specifically examine two concepts for measuring unemployment: the concept used by the German Federal Employment Agency (Bundesagentur für Arbeit, BA) and that of the International Labour Organization (ILO). Both

Table 5.1 Comparison of the BA and ILO concepts for measuring unemployment

	BA Concept	ILO Concept
Real phenomena	Unemployed persons	Economically inactive persons
Theoretical concept (Unemployment exists if...)	Less than 15 hours of work per week are performed	Less than one hour of work per week is performed
Measurable attributes	Registered individuals from the age of 15 up to the statutory retirement age (currently 65)	Surveyed individuals aged from the completed 15th year up to the completed 75th year of life
Measurement	Registration with the BA, a job center, or a municipal authority. This is a full census and a reference day value	Monthly telephone survey of the population. This is a sample survey and a monthly average
Data	Number of unemployed persons	Number of economically inactive persons

Table 5.2 Evaluation with regard to objectivity, reliability, and validity

	Criterion		
Method	Objectivity	Reliability	Validity
Interview	Only to a limited extent, as it depends on the person conducting the interview	Achieved if the interviewer uses a detailed interview guideline	Depends on the qualification of the person conducting the interview; might not be met with changing personnel
Quiz show	Yes, as random selection is independent of the conducting person	No, as different questions are asked on repetition	No, as the concept is not adequately captured
IQ test	Yes, as it is independent of the observer	Largely, as similar results are obtained upon repeated execution	Yes, if the test is suitable

concepts share the requirement that four criteria must be met for a person to be considered unemployed: lack of employment, ability to work, active job search, and availability on the labor market. However, when examining the different definitions and measurement methods of the two concepts, it becomes clear why they result in different figures for unemployment. The use of different terms such as unemployed versus economically inactive already points to differences in the delineation of the two indicators. Furthermore, the two approaches are based on different perspectives regarding underemployment: while the BA's perspective is also shaped by social policy considerations, the ILO primarily focuses on the immediate economic dimension.

2.2.3 The properties of data can be summarized under the three key points: objectivity, reliability, and validity. Objectivity refers to the independence of measurement results from the observer. Data is considered reliable when repeated measurements yield identical results, and validity means that the data actually describes or at least approximates real phenomena based on the given theoretical concept.

2.2.4 A summary evaluation of the three measurement methods with regard to the criteria of objectivity, reliability, and validity is provided in Table 5.2.

2.2.5 No sample solution.
Note: In your answer, refer to the various dimensions of data quality, which cannot easily be summarized into a one-dimensional indicator. Also explain why data quality depends on the intended application. Referring to a concrete example may be helpful.

2.2.6 No sample solution.

5.3 Data Processing

2.3.1 (a) The Laspeyres index is based on a basket of goods. The following assumptions are made: the weighting of the goods in the basket as well as the quality of the goods in the basket remain constant over time. A change in the Laspeyres price index compared to the respective base year is therefore attributed solely to a change in the prices of the goods in the basket, and not, for instance, to a change in the composition of the basket or to an improvement in the quality of the goods included in the basket. The advantage of the Laspeyres price index lies in its conceptual simplicity. The weights of the individual goods in the basket theoretically only need to be determined once, namely in the base year. Furthermore, the constant basket allows for good comparability of index levels with the same base year over time. In practice, however, the basket is regularly updated both in terms of the weights used and the goods considered, in order to remain representative of current consumption patterns.

The basket effect, also widely referred to as the substitution effect, is the tendency of the Laspeyres price index to overestimate a price increase. This tendency to overestimate the price increase is due to the assumption of constant weights for the goods in the basket, as it neglects the consumers' ability to substitute a good that has become more expensive with one that has remained price-stable or even become cheaper. For example, instead of buying more expensive apples, a consumer may purchase cheaper pears. As a result, their cost of living remains constant or even decreases, because they simply buy fewer apples and more pears. Due to the constant weights in the Laspeyres basket, this substitution from apples to pears is not taken into account, leading to a measured increase in the cost of living that is higher than the actual increase experienced by the consumer.

(b) The consideration of quality changes is of central importance for the calculation of price indices. In particular, technical goods, such as computers, undergo rapid development. Thus, it is impossible to observe the same goods over an extended period with unchanged quality. If the ongoing quality improvements were not accounted for in the calculation of price indices, this would lead to a distortion of the indices, typically resulting in an overestimation of the price increase. To avoid this distortion, so-called hedonic methods are employed in official statistics. This methods aim to carry out a quality adjustment, i.e., to adjust the price index for the price increase that can be explained by quality improvements. To do this, the good in question is conceptually broken down into its quality characteristics. In the case of a computer, these might include CPU performance, hard drive capacity, and RAM. Using regression analysis, the influence of these quality characteristics on the price of the computer is then determined. This makes it possible to adjust the changed price of the computer by excluding the price increase attributable, for example, to a doubling of the hard drive size.

(c) The use of hedonic price indices tends to lead to lower inflation rates, since quality improvements in this area are often greater than the unadjusted price increases recorded. For example, it can be observed that the price per gigabyte of hard drive storage has actually decreased over time. Economically, this corresponds to a price reduction.

The use of hedonic methods for measuring inflation is not valid if it is not possible to measure the influence of a good's quality characteristics on its price. This is the case, for instance, when prices are regulated by the state. An example in this context could be the capping of regional residential rental prices. In such a case, the rent of a dwelling is not determined solely by its location, insulation, or particularly advantageous layout, nor by the prices consumers are willing to pay for these quality features. In fact, the rent is set based on government regulations, making it impossible to measure the influence of quality characteristics on rental prices.

2.3.2 The following table presents the results for parts (a) and (c).

Year	2015	2016	2017	2018	2019	2020	2021	2022	2023	2024
$P^{CPI}_{2020=100}$	94.5	95.0	96.4	98.1	99.5	100.0	103.1	110.2	116.7	119.3
$P^{CPI}_{2015=100}$	100.0	100.5	102.0	103.8	105.3	105.8	109.1	116.6	123.5	126.3
Inflation %	-	0.53	1.47	1.76	1.43	0.50	3.10	6.89	5.90	2.23

Source: Federal Statistical Office; GENESIS-Online database; Table: 61111-0001

(b) Example calculation: $P^{CPI}_{2020=100}(2018) = \frac{103.81 \cdot 94.5}{100} = 98.1$

2.3.3 Table 5.3 presents the calculated "long series" of the German unit labor cost index. It is important to note that the index values with base year 1981 must each be divided by the value of this series from 1991 and then multiplied by 100, whereas the observations with base year 2015 must be divided by the 1991 value of that respective series. As a result, both series show an index value of 100 for the year 1991, allowing them to be linked.

2.3.4 No sample solution.

Solution hint: The calculation of annual growth rates can be done using the usual formula $\frac{x_t - x_{t-1}}{x_{t-1}}$ or as the difference of the natural logarithms of x_t and x_{t-1}. The comparison aims to determine whether wages or prices are rising faster. If logarithmic growth rates are used, the difference between the growth rate of wages and prices corresponds exactly to the development of real wages.

Table 5.3 Indices of Unit Labor Costs

Year	$I^{FRG}_{1991=100}$	Year	$I^{G}_{1991=100}$	Year	$I^{G}_{1991=100}$	Year	$I^{G}_{1991=100}$	Year	$I^{G}_{1991=100}$
1981	82.4	1991	100.0	2001	116.4	2011	124.1	2021	88.2
1982	85.8	1992	106.8	2002	117.4	2012	128.3	2022	92.1
1983	86.4	1993	111.3	2003	119.0	2013	131.0	2023	98.2
1984	87.2	1994	112.2	2004	118.4	2014	132.7	2024	103.7
1985	88.6	1995	114.8	2005	117.8	2015	135.4		
1986	90.9	1996	115.3	2006	115.0	2016	137.0		
1987	93.4	1997	114.2	2007	114.6	2017	138.5		
1988	93.7	1998	114.4	2008	117.6	2018	142.3		
1989	94.3	1999	115.5	2009	125.9	2019	146.9		
1990	96.5	2000	116.6	2010	123.9	2020	153.0		
1991	100.0								

Source: Council of Economic Experts and Federal Statistical Office; GENESIS-Online database; Table: 81000-0017

5.4 Economic Indicators

2.4.1 (a) The European Central Bank has declared price level stability as its central objective. It is seen as "the best contribution monetary policy can make to economic growth and job creation" (https://www.ecb.europa.eu/ecb/orga/tasks/monpol/html/index.en.html). Price stability is defined as an increase in the Harmonized Consumer Price Index (HCPI) compared to the previous year for the Eurozone of close to 2% over the medium term. In contrast to the former goal of the German Bundesbank, this target is considered to be a symmetric one. The European Central Bank considers inflation that is too low just as problematic as inflation that is too high.

A positive goal of about 2% is chosen to account for measurement inaccuracies in determining the HCPI, which might lead to an overestimation of the actual inflation rate. Examples include the basket effect, quality improvements of products, or the failure to consider sharply falling prices of newly introduced products. Since the considered HCPI also represents the average of the inflation rates of all Euro countries, an inflation rate target of 0% would imply that at least some countries would actually have to accept negative inflation rates (deflation), which is considered as a more challenging issues compared to moderate positive inflation rates.

(b) In macroeconomics, typically two measures are considered for calculating the price level: GDP deflator and consumer price index.

The GDP deflator P_t is intended to express the average price development for all economic activities included in the GDP. It is calculated as

$$P_t = \frac{\text{nominal GDP}}{\text{real GDP}}.$$

Thereby, the nominal GDP is calculated at the price level of the reporting year, whereas the real GDP is calculated at base year prices. Thus, the GDP deflator measures the price development between the current reporting year and the base year. Consequently, the inflation rate (π_t) for a period is given by

$$\pi_t = \frac{(P_t - P_{t-1})}{P_{t-1}}.$$

In contrast, a consumer price index measures the price development of selected consumer goods, i.e.

$$P_{0|t} = \sum_{i=1}^{n} w_i(t) \frac{p_i(t)}{p_i(0)},$$

where $p_i(0)$ and $p_i(t)$ denote the prices of good i ($i = 1, \ldots, n$) in the base year ($t = 0$) and the current period (t), respectively, while $w_i(t)$ is the weight of good i in period t. The price index can be calculated according to Laspeyres or Paasche. The difference between the two methods lies in the determination of the weights $w_i(t)$. In the approach proposed by Laspeyres, the weights are defined by the share of sales of good i in total sales in the base period 0, i.e.

$$w_i^{La}(t) = \sum_{i=1}^{n} \frac{p_i(0)q_i(0)}{\sum_{i=1}^{n} p_i(0)q_i(0)},$$

where $q_i(0)$ denotes the sales of good i in the base period.
In contrast, the weighting in the Paasche method is done by the share of sales of good i in period t

$$w_i^{Pa}(t) = \sum_{i=1}^{n} \frac{p_i(0)q_i(t)}{\sum_{i=1}^{n} p_i(0)q_i(t)},$$

where $q_i(t)$ denotes the sales of good i in period t.

(c) The basket effect describes an effect on the measurement of consumer price inflation. This arises from the fact that the Laspeyres index does not account for consumers' reactions to changes in relative prices in their consumption behavior. If consumers increasingly buy relatively cheaper goods, this has a dampening effect on the actual "experienced" inflation rate. Therefore, the inflation rate calculated on the basis of the Laspeyres index is considered as having a tendency to overestimate actual inflation rates.

2.4.2 Keyword "Employment Rate"

(a) The official unemployment rate u is defined as follows:

$$u = \frac{\text{registered unemployed}}{\text{labor force}}.$$

These are so-called "process data", which result from official unemployment reports of job-seeking persons. But how exactly are the numerator and denominator of the above quotient defined? Here is the corresponding information from the Federal Employment Agency regarding the term "registered unemployed":
"Unemployed persons according to §16 para. 2 SGB III are persons who,

1. are temporarily not employed or work less than 15 hours per week,
2. are seeking employment subject to compulsory insurance for at least 15 hours per week,
3. are available for placement efforts of the Employment Agency, i.e. are allowed, able and ready to work,
4. reside in Germany,
5. are not younger than 15 years and have not reached the retirement age year, and
6. have personally registered as unemployed at an Employment Agency."

Moreover, §16 para. 2 regulates that participants in active labor market policy measures are not considered unemployed (see also further explanations on the "definition of unemployment under SGB II and SGB III"—only in German language).[1] Conclusion: Not every individual unemployment report is actually included in the numerator of the officially reported unemployment rate.
For the denominator of the rate, the Federal Agency uses two different concepts (see also. "Calculation of unemployment rates and reference figures") [2]

1. Unemployment rate based on all civilian labor force: All civilian employed persons are the sum of dependent civilian employed persons as well as self-employed and assisting family members.
2. Unemployment rate based on dependent civilian labor force: The denominator contains only the dependent civilian employed persons, i.e. the sum

[1] https://statistik.arbeitsagentur.de/DE/Navigation/Grundlagen/Definitionen/Arbeitslosigkeit-Unterbeschaeftigung/Arbeitslosigkeit-Nav.html?submit=Suchen&templateQueryString=Arbeitslosenbegriff

[2] https://statistik.arbeitsagentur.de/DE/Navigation/Grundlagen/Definitionen/Berechnung-der-Arbeitslosenquote/Berechnung-der-Arbeitslosenquote-Nav.html

of employees subject to social insurance contributions (including trainees), marginally employed persons, and civil servants (excluding soldiers).

(b) An "tightness index" is understood as the ratio between the number of job seekers and the number of open vacancies. Thus, this measure can be interpreted as the average number of applicants per open position. However, such a view is greatly simplifying: the qualification heterogeneity of the job offers as well as the job seekers fundamentally questions the meaningfulness of an aggregated tightness index. But even with qualification compatibility between job seekers and job profiles, regional mismatch situations could cause a nationwide calculated tightness index to prove too coarse an approximation of the labor market situation. Furthermore, it must be pointed out that only a fraction of open vacancies are actually reported to the Federal Employment Agency. Therefore, a tightness index calculated based on officially reported vacancies will be biased and tend to show values that are too high.

(c) The overview just given shows that both concepts are afflicted with problems. However, the unemployment rate in principle seems suitable to depict the overall situation on the labor market. Besides the definitional peculiarities of the official unemployment statistics, the interpretation of this measure must also consider that the goal of a high employment level cannot generally be understood as a zero-percent unemployment rate. The necessary degree of unavoidable and thus tolerable unemployment, which arises for example due to changing jobs, seems difficult to determine.

2.4.3 (a) The unemployment rate can be used as an important instrument to assess the success of a government's labor market policy. However, there are limitations to the officially reported unemployment rate, as it does not include certain groups of people, e.g. those participating in labor market policy measures (even though they are also seeking employment during the participation period). Such measures include, for example, further training or targeted vocational reintegration. Therefore, the validity of the official unemployment rate as an indicator of the actual extent of underemployment, which could be relevant for electoral decisions, is limited.

(b) If the goal of the unemployment rate is to fully cover all persons who are actually unemployed in the usual sense of the word, then the applicant's objection is justified. Indeed, persons registered as jobseekers with the Federal Employment Agency who are not immediately available to the labor market are, by legal definition, not to be counted as unemployed (see §16 SGB III).

However, on the website of the Federal Employment Agency, at least for some relevant groups, additional figures are available—especially for those participating in labor market policy measures. This allows users to potentially apply alternative operationalizations of the unemployment rate.

(c) The number of unemployed persons according to the proposal would be higher than the reported rate, since many individuals involved in active and passive labor policy measures—including those not immediately available to the labor market—would be included in the calculation.

2.4.4 No sample solution.

2.4.5 Keyword "Business Cycle Indicators"

(a) A suitable indicator for assessing the current business cycle situation is the production index of the manufacturing industry, as it is the only concurrent indicator among those listed—i.e., a coincident indicator. It is thus the only one that reflects the current economic situation.

(b) In general, all other listed indicators can be classified as leading and trailing indicators, respectively. Leading indicators are forward-looking and provide clues about the future development of the economic situation. These include, for example, the stock index, which reflects expectations about future developments, and the order intake index, since orders should translate into future production. Trailing indicators, on the other hand, provide information about how the economy has developed in the past. The unemployment rate is a trailing indicator because, due to institutional factors, it takes time to lay off or hire workers in response to changes in production.

(c) The business cycle itself cannot be measured directly, as it is not an observable variable but rather a model-based construct. However, it is possible to measure various indicators that are strongly correlated with the concept of the business cycle and thus allow conclusions to be drawn about past, current, and future economic conditions. In principle, the following four criteria should be met by a suitable indicator:

- Plausibility: The indicator should be derived from a theory, i.e., there should be a theoretically justified relationship between the indicator and the reference variable.
- Statistical/data-related requirements: The data used to measure the indicator must be available, and there should be no (or only interpretable) structural breaks in the data.
- Conformity: The indicator should conform to past business cycles, i.e., its historical development should match the development of the reference variable. Furthermore, the time lag between the development of the indicator and the reference variable should be stable.
- Data timeliness: Especially if the indicator is used to forecast the reference variable, the available data must be up to date.

2.4.6 (a) Both ratios are calculated relative to gross domestic product (GDP). While the investment ratio is a true ratio, since investments are, by definition, a component of GDP, the social benefits ratio is a "pseudo" ratio, as social benefits are not a part of GDP.

(b) Therefore, the impression created by the graphical representation that higher values of the social benefits ratio must be associated with lower values of the investment ratio cannot be directly derived from any kind of balance mechanism. In addition, an analysis of economic interrelations would be necessary to plausibly argue that the two ratios are interdependent.

2.4.7 (a) For a given country, a positive output gap indicates that the actual production exceeds its (estimated) potential output, which typically occurs during the boom phase following an upswing.

(b) While no OECD member country exhibited a positive output gap in 2009, the increasing numbers, especially from 2014 onward, indicate a phase of economic expansion that had already transitioned into a boom phase in many of the countries considered by the end of the period.

2.4.8 (a) The concentration ratio CR_5 of the Eurozone is represented in each case by the left of the two columns.

(b) Despite a slight decline in 2015, there was a clear increase in the CR_5 concentration ratio in the Eurozone between 2005 and 2015. This means that, according to this indicator, concentration in the banking sector has risen significantly.

(c) The Herfindahl index is an absolute measure of concentration that also depends on the number of entities included in the analysis. The higher the Herfindahl index, the greater the concentration in the sector under consideration. This means that a few market participants account for a large share of the industry in question.

The observed increase in the Herfindahl index for the Eurozone from 2005 to 2015 (top line) indicates a rise in concentration and thus confirms the impression obtained using the CR_5 concentration ratio.

2.4.9 (a) The concentration ratio is an absolute measure of concentration. The concentration ratio CR_r shows the share of the r largest entities in the total sum of all entities. For the banking sector, CR_5 measures the share of bank assets held by the five largest banks relative to the total bank assets of all banks in the considered market.

(b) In Belgium, the concentration in the banking sector, as measured by the CR_5 concentration ratio, decreased significantly between 2008 (left column in each case) and 2014 (middle column), while there was no noticeable change between 2014 and 2015.

In contrast to Belgium, in Germany the concentration in the banking sector increased significantly between 2008 and 2014, and then declined only slightly between 2014 and 2015. The 2015 level is therefore clearly higher than in 2008. Overall, however, market concentration in Germany is lower in all considered years compared to the values reported for Belgium.

2.4.10 No sample solution.

2.4.11 No sample solution.

5.5 Input-Output Analysis

2.5.1 Three sector input-output table of the German economy

(a) No sample solution.

(b) The production values of the individual sectors ($\mathbf{X}$) can be determined as a function of the components of final demand ($\mathbf{Y}$) using the Leontief inverse ($(\mathbf{I} - \mathbf{A})^{-1}$):

$$\mathbf{X} = (\mathbf{I} - \mathbf{A})^{-1}\mathbf{Y}\,.$$

(c) The Leontief model

- The Leontief model assumes the input coefficients to be constant. Therefore, it is suited for static analysis, i.e., in the short-run, and small changes of output volumes, when the assumption of a constant technology might be adequate. In addition, a linearly homogeneous production technology is assumed:

$$X_{ij} = \alpha_{ij} \cdot X_j \quad \text{for } i, j = 1, \ldots, n\,.$$

  Thus, it is assumed that the input coefficients are constant not only over time but also with respect to the volume of production.
- The production function considered is the linear Leontief production function. From an economic perspective, it should be critically noted that
  - relative price changes, by assumption, do not induce any substitution of intermediate inputs. At least for short-term and sufficiently small changes, however, this assumption may be valid. Consider, for example, an automobile manufacturer: if it wants to increase its output in the short term, this results in a model-specific fixed additional demand for aluminum, plastics, steel, etc. Only in the medium term, i.e., after the development of new models, is the manufacturer able to react to changed input prices and substitute individual inputs.
  - the failure to consider the investment activities of companies, as exemplified above, also excludes any technical progress from the analysis.

Consequently, for a long-term perspective, the static modeling approach of standard input-output analysis is not well suited. For that purpose, corresponding dynamic extensions are a better choice. For short- to medium-term analysis horizons, however, the assumption of constant input coefficients can at least be justified approximately.

- To calculate the (rounded) Leontief inverse:

$$(I - A) = \begin{pmatrix} 0,89 & -0,01 & 0,00 \\ -0,14 & 0,67 & -0,07 \\ -0,14 & -0,15 & 0,68 \end{pmatrix}$$

$$\Rightarrow (I - A)^{-1} = \begin{pmatrix} 1,13 & 0,02 & 0,00 \\ 0,27 & 1,53 & 0,16 \\ 0,29 & 0,34 & 1,51 \end{pmatrix}$$

(d)

$$\Delta Y = (I - A) \cdot \Delta X$$

$$\Rightarrow \Delta Y = \begin{pmatrix} 0,89 & -0,01 & 0,00 \\ -0,14 & 0,67 & -0,07 \\ -0,14 & -0,15 & 0,68 \end{pmatrix} \begin{pmatrix} -1,00 \\ 0,00 \\ 1,00 \end{pmatrix} = \begin{pmatrix} -0,89 \\ 0,07 \\ 0,82 \end{pmatrix}$$

(e)

$$\Delta X = (I - A)^{-1} \cdot \Delta Y$$

$$= \begin{pmatrix} 1,13 & 0,02 & 0,00 \\ 0,27 & 1,53 & 0,16 \\ 0,29 & 0,34 & 1,51 \end{pmatrix} \begin{pmatrix} 0,00 \\ 0,00 \\ 50,00 \end{pmatrix} = \begin{pmatrix} 0,00 \\ 8,00 \\ 75,00 \end{pmatrix}$$

2.5.2 (a) $V_{1,1} = 20$ indicates that the agriculture sector consumes 20 units of goods from within the agriculture sector itself as intermediate inputs to produce its total output of 50 units. An example of such intermediate inputs within the agriculture sector could be the supply of seeds between agricultural production enterprises. $V_{2,1} = 11$ indicates that the industry sector supplies 11 units of goods as intermediate products to the agriculture sector. An example of this could be agricultural machinery such as tractors.

(b) • $b(1,1) = \frac{X(1,1)}{\sum_{j=1}^{4} X(1,j)} = \frac{20}{50} = 0.4$, i.e., 40% of the agricultural goods produced are needed again as input for agricultural production itself.

- $b(1,2) = \frac{X(1,2)}{\sum_{j=1}^{4} X(1,j)} = \frac{4}{50} = 0.08$, i.e., 8% of the agricultural goods produced are passed on as intermediate inputs to the industry sector.
- $b(1,4) = \frac{X(1,4)}{\sum_{j=1}^{4} X(1,j)} = \frac{19}{50} = 0.38$, i.e., 38% of the agricultural goods go to final consumption.

(c)
- $a(1,2) = \frac{X(1,2)}{\sum_{i=1}^{4} X(i,2)} = \frac{4}{100} = 0.04$, i.e., intermediate inputs from agriculture account for 4% of the total inputs in the industry sector.
- $a(2,1) = \frac{X(2,1)}{\sum_{i=1}^{4} X(i,1)} = \frac{11}{50} = 0.22$, i.e., intermediate inputs from the industry sector account for 22% of the total inputs in the agriculture sector, or in other words: 22% of the production costs in agriculture are due to intermediate inputs from the industry sector.
- $a(4,1) = \frac{X(4,1)}{\sum_{i=1}^{4} X(i,1)} = \frac{14}{50} = 0.28$, i.e., 28% of the costs in the agriculture sector arise from labor or its remuneration.

(d)

$$A = \begin{pmatrix} a(1,1) & \cdots & a(1,3) \\ a(2,1) & \ddots & \vdots \\ a(3,1) & \cdots & a(3,3) \end{pmatrix} = \begin{pmatrix} \cdots & 0.04 & \cdots \\ 0.22 & \ddots & \vdots \\ \cdots & \cdots & \cdots \end{pmatrix}$$

5.6 The Econometric Model

2.6.1 The general procedure for implementing an econometric model can be described by the following four steps:

1. Specification of the model
2. Estimation of the parameters
3. Examination of the estimated model
4. Evaluation and interpretation of the results

2.6.2 An "econometric model" generally refers to a relationship between economic variables that can be formally represented using mathematical notation, and for which a theoretically justified causal link exists. The parameters of the model can, in principle, be quantified, that is, assigned specific numerical values. Moreover, an econometric model allows statements regarding the statistical properties of the parameter estimates.

A typical example would be the influence of years of education on wage levels. Let W_i denote the hourly wage (in Euros) of the person i, and A_i their duration of education (in years). Then, a simple formal model might look as follows:

$$W_i = \beta_1 + \beta_2 A_i + \varepsilon_i$$

- Here, the "dependent variable" W_i is the variable the model seeks to explain. The focus is on what determines the level of this variable.
- The "explanatory variable" in this model is A_i. This variable is not explained within the model, but is assumed to be given, which is why it is also referred to as an "independent variable". A model often includes several explanatory variables. For example, in addition to education, the age of the person i could also influence wage levels.
- The "functional form" describes the function that characterizes the relationship between the variables in the model. Often, the choice of this function is based on a priori assumption. In the example, it might be assumed that it is a simple linear relationship or that a linear relationship is at least a good approximation.
- Since the actual level of the dependent variable generally cannot be entirely explained by the explanatory variable(s) alone, the econometric model includes a "disturbance term" (also named "erorr term"), which captures the effects of all other factors not explicitly included in the model. It is often denoted by ε_i. In the specific example, influences such as work experience, sector, or region would be captured in the error term since they are not an explicit part of the model.

2.6.3 The assumption of the functional relationship and the distribution of the error process play a central role in the estimation procedures applied in econometrics. Although systematic effects are captured through the independent variable X, the model is extended by a random component ε_t to account for the influence of omitted or unknown factors. This component is also known as the "disturbance term" or "error term". An essential part of evaluating the estimation is therefore to examine to what extent the initial assumptions about the model and its error terms are actually fulfilled. Since ε_t is not observable, the assumptions are tested using the estimated residuals $\widehat{\varepsilon_t}$. For example, incorrect assumptions regarding the functional form or the omission of relevant variables will be reflected in the residuals $\widehat{\varepsilon_t}$. This affects all subsequent phases of the analysis and can lead to quantitative and qualitative distortions of the results. Various testing procedures are available to review the assumptions made.

5.7 The Linear Regression Model

2.7.1 A key observation is that the income tax rate in Germany is not linear but instead prescribes different marginal tax rates for different levels of income. The initially intuitive modeling

$$\text{Tax}_i = \beta_0 + \beta_1 \text{Income}_i + \varepsilon_i$$

is therefore a misspecification, as β_1 assumes a constant marginal tax rate. The actual tax rate, which due to a multitude of exemptions, deductions, etc., can only be represented with great effort, could, for example, be approximated by a quadratic function that at least allows for some degree of progression, i.e.

$$\text{Tax}_i = \beta_0 + \beta_1 \text{Income}_i + \beta_2 \text{Income}_i^2 + \varepsilon_i \,.$$

The marginal effect of an increase in income on income tax can no longer be directly read off from β_1. Rather, for the marginal tax rate in this model, the following holds:

$$\frac{\partial \text{Tax}}{\partial \text{Income}} = \beta_1 + 2\beta_2 \text{Income} \,.$$

If β_2 is positive, then the marginal tax rate increases with income.

2.7.2 (a) The coefficient for lnD can be interpreted as an elasticity, since both the dependent and the explanatory variable are used in natural logarithmic form. This means that an increase in the distance to the waste incineration plant by 1% leads to an increase in house prices by approximately 0.321%. Since a waste incineration plant in the immediate vicinity is likely to reduce the attractiveness of a residential property, the positive sign corresponds to the expectation that house prices increase with greater distance from the plant.

(b) First of all, the relationship chosen here is a strong simplification, since many other factors are likely to influence house prices (see part (d)). Moreover, the city administration may choose less attractive city areas for building a waste incineration plant, expecting less resistance there. Thus, a waste incineration plant is most likely to be built on the outskirts of the city and not in the city center, and therefore has a greater distance from the more expensive residential areas. Causality could therefore—at least partially—run in the opposite direction.

(c) The R^2 of 0.162 indicates that 16.2% of the variance in house prices can be explained by the variable lnD. This seems quite considerable for the single variable of distance to a waste incineration plant. At the same time, however, the value suggests that there are still a number of other important factors that could be used to model differences in house prices.

(d) Other influencing factors on house prices include, for example, the age of the house, as well as the lot size and living space. Distances to the city center, to the nearest supermarket, or to leisure facilities are also likely to be important. At least for the distance to the city center, there may be a correlation with the distance to a waste incineration plant (see (b)).

2.7.3 (a) As the method of least squares, we refer to a formal approach for fitting a straight line—or in the multivariate model, a hyperplane—to a given dataset. At this point, we will restrict ourselves to the illustrative case of a bivariate relationship

$y_i = f(x_i)$. Given observations $\{(y_1, x_1), \ldots, (y_n, x_n)\}$, the aim is to fit a line of the form

$$\hat{y}_i = \hat{\beta}_0 + \hat{\beta}_1 x_i$$

"as well as possible" to the observed data. The criterion used to determine the goodness of fit is based on the resulting deviations (residuals) between the observed values $\{y_1, \ldots, y_n\}$ and the values computed (predicted) using the regression line $\{\hat{y}_1, \ldots, \hat{y}_n\}$:

$$\hat{\varepsilon}_i = y_i - \hat{y}_i \,.$$

To optimize the fit, the method of least squares minimizes the sum of these squared deviations. The specific form of the line is chosen such that

$$\sum_{i=1}^{n} \hat{\varepsilon}_i^2$$

is minimized, whereby the parameter estimates $\hat{\beta}_0$ (intercept) and $\hat{\beta}_1$ (slope parameter) are determined numerically.
If this linear approach is justified, i.e., if the dataset under consideration was in fact generated by a relationship of the form

$$y_i = \beta_0 + \beta_1 x_i + \varepsilon_i$$

and if the variable x truly "explains" the development of the variable y, is not stochastic or not correlated with the stochastic error terms ε, and has finite variance, then this method allows the unknown parameters β_0 and β_1 to be estimated without bias. The property of unbiasedness follows from the assumption of unsystematic error terms, i.e., from the assumed condition

$$E[\varepsilon_i] = 0 \,.$$

In the econometric model, it is furthermore typically assumed that the variance of the error terms remains constant over time

$$VAR[\varepsilon_i] = \sigma^2 \,,$$

the error terms are uncorrelated with each other, and they follow a normal distribution. The estimates $\hat{\beta}_0$ and $\hat{\beta}_1$ then also follow a normal distribution and are efficient, meaning that the OLS method provides unbiased estimators with minimal variance. The estimates are still normally distributed at least asymptotically, when the error terms do not follow exactly a normal distribution.

(b) Among the desirable properties of estimators $\hat{\beta}$ are in particular:

- **Unbiasedness**: $E(\hat{\beta}) = \beta$, i.e., with repeated applications of the analysis using different random samples, the expected value of the estimated parameter equals the true parameter value β. There are therefore no systematic biases, which are naturally undesirable.
- **Consistency**: $plim_{T \to \infty} \hat{\beta} = \beta$, i.e., as the sample size T increases, the estimated value increasingly approximates the true parameter value.
- **Efficiency**: The estimator has the smallest variance among all considered unbiased estimators, i.e., the differences in estimates for different samples are as small as possible for the given sample size.
- **Normality**: The distribution of the parameter estimators, which are themselves random variables as functions of the error terms, follows a normal distribution. This greatly facilitates hypothesis testing, especially for small samples.

These properties are exhibited by OLS estimators when a set of assumptions—particularly concerning the distribution of the model's error terms—is satisfied.

(c) The general case of the linear regression model with k explanatory variables can be represented by the following equation:

$$Y_t = \beta_1 + \beta_2 X_{2t} + \beta_3 X_{3t} + \ldots + \beta_k X_{kt} + \varepsilon_t \qquad t = 1, \ldots, T$$

Three categories of assumptions can be distinguished:

1. Assumptions about the model:

- The true relationship between X and Y is linear.
- No relevant exogenous variables are omitted.
- Linearity in the parameters holds.

2. Assumptions about the regressors:

- The elements of the matrix X are deterministic (non-stochastic), or it holds that $E(X_i \varepsilon_i) = 0$.
- The variance of the exogenous variables is finite.
- X has full column rank k.

3. Assumptions about the error terms:

- $E(\varepsilon) = 0$
- $Var(\varepsilon) = E(\varepsilon_i \varepsilon_i') = \sigma_\varepsilon^2 \mathbf{I}$

- $Cov(\varepsilon_i, \varepsilon_j) = 0$ for $i \neq j$
- For exact inference in finite samples, it is additionally required that the random variables ε follow a normal distribution.

2.7.4 1st Step: Minimization of the sum of squared residuals. For this, the expression on the right-hand side is minimized, i.e. partial derivatives with respect to both $\hat{\beta}$ coefficients are taken.

$$\sum_{t=1}^{T} \hat{\epsilon}_t^2 = \sum_{t=1}^{T} (y_t - \hat{\beta}_1 - \hat{\beta}_2 x_t)^2$$

2nd Step: Set the partial derivative with respect to $\hat{\beta}_1$ equal to zero.

$$\begin{aligned}
\frac{\partial \sum_{t=1}^{T} \hat{\epsilon}_t^2}{\partial \hat{\beta}_1} &= \sum_{t=1}^{T} 2(y_t - \hat{\beta}_1 - \hat{\beta}_2 x_t)(-1) = 0 \\
2(-1) \sum_{t=1}^{T} (y_t - \hat{\beta}_1 - \hat{\beta}_2 x_t) &= 0 \\
\sum_{t=1}^{T} (y_t - \hat{\beta}_1 - \hat{\beta}_2 x_t) &= 0 \\
\sum_{t=1}^{T} y_t - \sum_{t=1}^{T} \hat{\beta}_1 - \sum_{t=1}^{T} \hat{\beta}_2 x_t &= 0 \\
\sum_{t=1}^{T} y_t - T\hat{\beta}_1 - \sum_{t=1}^{T} \hat{\beta}_2 x_t &= 0 \\
\text{with } \overline{y} = \frac{1}{T} \sum_{t=1}^{T} y_t, \overline{x} = \frac{1}{T} \sum_{t=1}^{T} x_t \Rightarrow \overline{y} - \hat{\beta}_1 - \hat{\beta}_2 \overline{x} &= 0 \\
\Rightarrow \hat{\beta}_1 &= \overline{y} - \hat{\beta}_2 \overline{x}
\end{aligned}$$

3rd Step: Set the partial derivative with respect to $\hat{\beta}_2$ equal to zero.

$$\begin{aligned}
\frac{\partial \sum_{t=1}^{T} \hat{\epsilon}_t^2}{\partial \hat{\beta}_2} &= \sum_{t=1}^{T} 2(y_t - \hat{\beta}_1 - \hat{\beta}_2 x_t)(-x_t) = 0 \\
2(-1) \sum_{t=1}^{T} (y_t - \hat{\beta}_1 - \hat{\beta}_2 x_t) x_t &= 0
\end{aligned}$$

$$\sum_{t=1}^{T}(y_t - \hat{\beta}_1 - \hat{\beta}_2 x_t)x_t = 0$$

$$\sum_{t=1}^{T} y_t x_t - \sum_{t=1}^{T} \hat{\beta}_1 x_t - \sum_{t=1}^{T} \hat{\beta}_2 x_t x_t = 0$$

$$\sum_{t=1}^{T} x_t y_t - \sum_{t=1}^{T} \hat{\beta}_1 x_t - \sum_{t=1}^{T} \hat{\beta}_2 x_t^2 = 0$$

$$\overline{x \cdot y} - \hat{\beta}_1 \overline{x} - \hat{\beta}_2 \overline{x^2} = 0$$

$$\overline{x \cdot y} - (\overline{y} - \hat{\beta}_2 \overline{x})\overline{x} - \hat{\beta}_2 \overline{x^2} = 0$$

$$\overline{x \cdot y} - \overline{x} \cdot \overline{y} + \hat{\beta}_2 \overline{x} \cdot \overline{x} - \hat{\beta}_2 \overline{x^2} = 0$$

$$\overline{x \cdot y} - \overline{x} \cdot \overline{y} = \hat{\beta}_2 \overline{x^2} - \hat{\beta}_2 \overline{x}^2$$

$$\hat{\beta}_2(\overline{x^2} - \overline{x}^2) = \overline{x \cdot y} - \overline{x} \cdot \overline{y}$$

$$\Rightarrow \hat{\beta}_2 = \frac{\overline{x \cdot y} - \overline{x} \cdot \overline{y}}{\overline{x^2} - \overline{x}^2}$$

2.7.5 Estimation of a macroeconomic consumption function.

(a) The model can be written as follows:

$$CONSUMPTION_t = \beta_0 + \beta_1 \cdot DISP\_INC_t + \varepsilon_t \,,$$

or, following the usual theoretical style:

$$Y_t = \beta_0 + \beta_1 \cdot X_t + \varepsilon_t \,,$$

or finally with the estimated parameter values:

$$\hat{C}_t = 2.0482 + 0.8864 Y_t^d \,.$$

(b) The equation above is found in every introductory textbook on macroeconomic theory. There, you will find that the coefficient β_1 can be interpreted as the "marginal propensity to consume".
The substantive interpretation based on the current estimation result becomes: If disposable household income increases by one billion Euros, private consumption increases by approximately 0.8864 billion Euros or 886.4 million Euros.

(c) The t-statistic to be calculated for the null hypothesis ($H_0 : \beta_{1,0} = 1$) is:

$$
\begin{aligned}
t &= \frac{\hat{\beta}_1 - \beta_{1,0}}{\hat{\sigma}_{\hat{\beta}_1}} \\
&= \frac{(0.886359 - 1)}{0.012614} \\
&= -9.0091
\end{aligned}
$$

For a two-sided test at the 5% level, the corresponding critical value is: $t_{0.975} = 1.96$. Since $|-9.0091| > 1.96$, the tested hypothesis can therefore be rejected. However, this conclusion should be treated with caution without prior verification of the model assumptions.

(d) The coefficient of determination is defined as

$$
R^2 = \frac{ESS}{TSS} = 1 - \frac{RSS}{TSS}
$$

and thus describes the proportion of the variation in the dependent variable explained by the econometric model. A large part of the variation in consumption (more than 97%) is captured by the variation in income.

2.7.6 (a) The model to be estimated

$$
\text{Tax}_i = \beta_1 + \beta_2 \text{Income}_i + \beta_3 \text{Income}_i^2 + \varepsilon_i \, ,
$$

or the estimated model

$$
\text{Tax}_i = \hat{\beta}_1 + \hat{\beta}_2 \text{Income}_i + \hat{\beta}_3 \text{Income}_i^2 + \hat{\varepsilon}_i
$$

or the model prediction

$$
\widehat{\text{Tax}}_i = \hat{\beta}_1 + \hat{\beta}_2 \text{Income}_i + \hat{\beta}_3 \text{Income}_i^2
$$

(b) To calculate the expected income tax, the model prediction is used, where the parameter estimates $\hat{\beta}_k$ are replaced by their respective numerical values, and income is set to the assumed value of 100,000€:

$$
\begin{aligned}
& E(\text{Tax}|\text{Income} = 100,000) && (5.1) \\
&= -1485.182 + 0.2306 \cdot 100,000 + 0.14 \cdot 10^{-6} \cdot 100,000^2 && (5.2) \\
&= 35,577.02 \, . && (5.3)
\end{aligned}
$$

(c) The coefficient $1.40 \cdot 10^{-6}$ on the variable Income^2 reflects an increasing marginal tax rate, since with rising income, not only does each additional euro lead to 0.23 euro more in taxes via coefficient $\hat{\beta}_2$, but also an additional amount increasing with income due to the quadratic form via coefficient $\hat{\beta}_3$.

(d) The t-statistic for the null hypothesis $H_0 : \beta_3 = 0$ is 433.3426 and thus far exceeds the critical value at the 5% level, so the null hypothesis can be rejected. This is also reflected by the reported marginal p-value, which is well below 0.05.

(e) The R^2 statistic indicates that approximately 98% of the variation in income tax can be explained by the quadratic form of taxable income. While this is a very high value, it should be noted that the exact course of the tax function is legally defined, so a perfect fit would be theoretically possible, but not achievable with a quadratic function.

2.7.7 (a) The model to be estimated

$$M_t = \beta_1 + \beta_2 P_t + \varepsilon_t ,$$

or the estimated model

$$M_t = \hat{\beta}_1 + \hat{\beta}_2 P_t + \hat{\varepsilon}_t$$

or the model forecast

$$\widehat{M}_t = \hat{\beta}_1 + \hat{\beta}_2 P_t ,$$

where M could also be replaced by the specific definition ln(M3) and P by ln(GDP-deflator).

(b) Since both the dependent variable and the coefficient of the price level are in logarithmic form, the parameters can be interpreted as elasticities. In particular, β_2 is the price elasticity of the money supply, i.e., an increase in prices by 1% would lead to a growth of the money supply by β_2 percent, i.e., by approximately 3.68%.

(c) The t-statistic corresponding to the null hypothesis $H_0 : \beta_1 = 0$ can be read directly from the estimation output. Its value is -4.5223. Therefore, the absolute value of the t-statistic is well above the critical value at the 5% level of 1.968, so the null hypothesis must be rejected. Hence, the constant is significantly different from zero.

(d) For the null hypothesis $H_0 : \beta_{2,0} = 3$, the relevant t-statistic is not reported. However, it can be calculated using the available information:

$$t\text{-Stat} = \frac{\hat{\beta}_2 - \beta_{2,0}}{\hat{\sigma}_{\hat{\beta}_2}} = \frac{3.6774 - 3}{0.1643} = 4.1229$$

Since the absolute value of the test statistic is greater than the critical value, the null hypothesis must be rejected.

2.7.8 (a) The coefficient for C corresponds to the estimate $\hat{\beta}_1$ for β_1. This indicates the y-intercept of the regression line, i.e., the crime rate that would be expected if zero police officers were working in the district. The result is approximately 62 crimes per 1000 inhabitants. The coefficient is significantly different from 0 at the 5% level (t-statistic well above 1.968 or—equivalently—p-value well below 0.05).
The coefficient of POLPC is the estimated value for β_2. This shows that for each additional police officer per 1000 inhabitants, the crime rate is estimated to increase by 17 crimes per 1000 inhabitants. The coefficient is also clearly significantly different from 0 at the 5% level (t-statistic well above 1.968 or p-value well below 0.05).

(b) As a direct recommendation, one might conclude that the number of police officers should be reduced as much as possible—in principle down to zero. The model would then predict the lowest expected crime rate. At first glance, however, this conclusion appears to contradict intuition.

(c) First of all, it should be noted that a regression model only captures conditional correlation, not causality directly. In this particular case, reverse causality could be present—for instance, if more police officers are deployed in districts with higher crime rates. In that case, the explanatory variable POLPC would itself be endogenous, as it depends on the dependent variable CRMRTE.
Another issue could arise from the measurement of the crime rate. If it is based on cases recorded by the police, it stands to reason that the measured rate could rise with more police officers, even if the actual rate does not necessarily change. In this case, only the so-called "estimated number of unrecorded cases" would decrease. Such problems are commonly discussed under the term "measurement error".
Finally, a number of important explanatory factors are missing that may also influence the crime rate and possibly correlate with the number of deployed police officers. The absence of further variables is indicated by the R^2 value of 0.1343, which shows that only about 13% of the variation in the crime rate can be explained by the correlation with the number of police officers. As an example of missing variables, one might consider Vatican City, which, despite having very high security measures (many deployed police officers), reports a high crime rate. Both of these high values can be explained by the large number of tourists, which may attract pickpockets.

5.8 Residual Analysis and Check of Model Assumptions

2.8.1 (a) The model can be written as follows:

$$ln(\text{M3}_t) = \beta_0 + \beta_1 \cdot ln(\text{BIP}_t) + \beta_2 \cdot ln(\text{R}_t) + \varepsilon_t \,.$$

Alternatively, you could write down the estimated model.

(b) Since the elements of the function are logarithms, the coefficient β_1 represents the income elasticity of money demand. In this case, it means that an increase in GDP by 1% leads to an increase in the money supply M3 by approximately 1.19%.

(c) The Durbin-Watson statistic enables testing for first-order autocorrelation of the error terms (H_0: there is no first-order autocorrelation).
For the estimated model, the value is DW $=$ 1.3701. Since DW $<$ 1.6, the null hypothesis must be rejected at the 5% level, and first-order (positive) autocorrelation should be assumed.

(d) The introduction of the euro (initially as a unit of account) in January 1999 leads to a structural break. Afterwards, it becomes difficult to distinguish between national money supplies with the Euro zone in terms of their use as a means of transaction.

2.8.2 (a) The strictest assumptions for applying the t- and F-tests in statistical inference are those stated in the exercies, i.e.,

(1) Constant variance of the error terms, i.e. $Var(\varepsilon_t) = \sigma_t \equiv \sigma$. This means, for example, that the (absolute) size of the error terms should not systematically increase or decrease over time.

(2) The error terms ε_t and ε_s for different observations $t \neq s$ should be independent, i.e., in particular not correlated. This means, for example, that there should not be prolonged periods with only positive or only negative error terms.

(3) The error terms ε_t should follow a normal distribution with mean 0 and variance σ^2, i.e., $\varepsilon \sim \mathcal{N}(0, \sigma^2)$. This assumption is often justified because the error terms summarize a variety of small influences, so the central limit theorem may apply. However, this is not always the case.

If not all assumptions are met, both the ordinary least squares estimation and the calculation of the t- and F-statistics can still be performed. However, the least squares estimation may then lose its desirable properties such as unbiasedness, consistency, and efficiency. Moreover, in this case, the calculated t- and F-statistics no longer necessarily follow the t- or F-distribution, meaning that critical values from the respective distribution tables cannot be used. Thus, the usual procedure for testing a null hypothesis like $\beta_2 = 0$ using the corresponding t-statistic and the critical values from the t-distribution table is no longer valid.

Since the error terms ε_t are not observable, all procedures to test the mentioned properties are based on the estimated residuals $\hat{\varepsilon}_t$.

(b) The null hypothesis that the error terms are normally distributed can be tested using the Jarque-Bera statistic. The statistic is based on a comparison of the empirical skewness and kurtosis of the residuals with those of a normal distribution (skewness: 0, kurtosis: 3). If the statistic takes large values, it indicates that the empirical distribution significantly deviates in shape from a normal distribution. The null hypothesis of normality is rejected at the 5% level if the test statistic exceeds 5.99 (the 95%-quantile of the χ^2 distribution with 2 degrees of freedom).

(c) One test to verify the null hypothesis of constant variance is the White test. This involves trying to explain the squared residuals $\hat{\varepsilon}_t^2$ by the explanatory variables of the model, their squares, and interaction terms (in the case of multiple explanatory variables). If all these factors jointly have explanatory power, which can be determined using an F-test, this is a clear indication of non-constant variance, and the null hypothesis must be rejected.

(d) Dependence of the error terms usually has the most severe effects on estimation and inference. Therefore, there are several procedures for testing the null hypothesis of independence for various use cases. The simplest procedure—though only testing for first-order autocorrelation (i.e., whether ε_t and ε_{t-1} are correlated) and not suitable for dynamic models—is the Durbin-Watson test based on the Durbin-Watson statistic, which is calculated from the residuals $\hat{\varepsilon}_t$. The critical values for this statistic also depend on the actual observations, so they cannot be given universally. However, in practice, it is common to reject the null hypothesis "no first-order autocorrelation" at the 5% level if the Durbin-Watson statistic DW is below 1.6 or above 2.4. The acceptance region is therefore the interval [1.6; 2.4].

(e) Autocorrelation of the error terms is primarily a problem in the analysis of time series or spatially structured data. Typical causes include the omission of important explanatory variables, structural breaks, or incorrect functional form. If an important explanatory variable is missing, its effect will appear in the error term. If it is an economic variable such as the interest rate in a consumption function, it is often itself time-dependent, which transfers into the error term. Structural breaks, both in the form of sudden level shifts of the dependent variable or changes in the slope parameter, also lead to prolonged phases where the error terms have the same sign. A similar pattern emerges if, for example, a truly quadratic relationship is modeled using a linear regression line.

2.8.3 (a) The Durbin-Watson test is used to test the null hypothesis that the residuals do not exhibit first-order autocorrelation. For this, an AR(1) process is assumed for the error terms:

$$\varepsilon_t = \rho\varepsilon_{t-1} + v_t$$

Here, v_t is an independently normally distributed random variable. The test statistic for the residuals $\widehat{\varepsilon_t}$ is given by:

$$DW = \frac{\sum_{t=1}^{T} \hat{\varepsilon}_t - \hat{\varepsilon}_t}{\sum_{t=1}^{T} \hat{\varepsilon}_{t-1}}$$

Exact critical values for DW depend on the coefficients. Therefore, a rule of thumb is that the null hypothesis ($\rho = 0$) must be rejected at a 5% significance level if DW is less than 1.6 or greater than 2.4. Accordingly, in the model considered here, the null hypothesis cannot be rejected. This is not a surprising result, as this is a cross-sectional analysis for the year 2001, and thus no autocorrelation of the residuals is expected.

(b) Under the null hypothesis of normality, the Jarque-Bera statistic follows an asymptotic χ^2 distribution with two degrees of freedom. In this case, the null hypothesis can be rejected at the 1% level, as $2.82 \cdot 10^9$ clearly exceeds the critical value of 9.21. The null hypothesis of "normally distributed error terms" must therefore be rejected.

(c) In this case, the squared residuals were regressed on the squared explanatory variables and their cross-products. This is the White test, which is used to test the null hypothesis of homoskedastic residuals.
Using the F-test, it can be checked whether the null hypothesis $\beta_2 = \beta_3 = \beta_4 = \beta_5 = 0$ (i.e. all coefficients but the constant are zero) must be rejected. In this example, the F-statistic is $F = 3247.95$. Thus, the null hypothesis can be rejected, and the error terms do not exhibit constant variance.

2.8.4 (a) The coefficient of the logarithm of per capita income has a positive sign. An increase in per capita income by 1%, i.e., an increase in `LOG GDP` by 0.01, would therefore, ceteris paribus, lead to an increase in the Happiness Score by $0.125 \cdot 0.01$ units. However, this effect is not statistically significantly different from zero, as can be seen from the t-statistic of 1.1609.
The life expectancy (`LIFE EXPECTANCY`) is measured in years and also shows a positive sign. An increase in life expectancy by one year would thus lead to an increase in the Happiness Score by 0.0506 units. According to the t-statistic of 3.2122 and the corresponding p-value (`Prob.`), this effect is significantly different from zero at the 5% and even the 1% level.

(b) The Durbin-Watson statistic allows testing for first-order autocorrelation. In the present regression, the value is DW=1.627991, which means that the null hypothesis of no first-order autocorrelation cannot be rejected. This result is also in line with expectations, since the present regression is a cross-sectional analysis and not a time series analysis. The countries in the sample were alphabetically ordered, so autocorrelation would only arise if countries with similar initial letters exhibited similar deviations from the estimated regression equation.

(c) On the x-axis of the graph, the values for SOCIAL_SUPPORT of the countries considered are plotted. For each observed level of social support, the corresponding estimated residuals RESID are plotted on the y-axis. Upon closer inspection, a cone narrowing towards the top right can be observed. The deviations from the estimated regression equation thus appear to decrease as social support increases. This suggests a negative relationship between the Happiness Score and the variance of the residuals. Hence, there is reason to suspect that the error terms are heteroskedastic. This should be checked with a formal test.

(d) The White test conducted here tests the null hypothesis: "The error terms are homoskedastic." Upon closer inspection, the stated degrees of freedom (6) indicate that the version of the test without cross-products was used.
In the present example, the F-statistic is 3.123. From the p-value given after F(6,119)—which is below 0.05—it can be concluded that the null hypothesis must be rejected at the 5% level. Thus, the residuals do not exhibit constant variance. As a result, inference statements are not based on correct distributional assumptions, and the estimation of the variance of the estimated parameters may be biased.

5.9 Qualitative Variables

2.9.1 (a) There is perfect **multicollinearity**. The dummy variables worker, employee, and civil servant are perfectly correlated and can be represented by the following linear combination:

$$1 = \texttt{WORKER}_i + \texttt{EMPLOYEE}_i + \texttt{OFFICIAL}_i$$

As a consequence, the OLS estimator $\hat{\beta}$ can no longer be computed unambiguously by the standard formula, since the matrix $\boldsymbol{X}'\boldsymbol{X}$ is singular and therefore not invertible. The estimates are not identified.

(b) In order to estimate this model nonetheless, either (i) the constant or (ii) one of the perfectly multicollinear dummy variables must be omitted.
(i) without constant

$$\begin{aligned}\texttt{WAGE}_i &= \alpha_1 \text{SCHOOL}_i + \alpha_2 \text{AGE}_i + \alpha_3 \texttt{Worker}_i \\ &\quad + \alpha_4 \texttt{EMPLOYEE}_i + \alpha_5 \texttt{OFFICIAL}_i + \varepsilon_i\end{aligned}$$

(ii) without dummy variable Civil Servant

$$\begin{aligned}\texttt{WAGE}_i &= \alpha_0 + \alpha_1 \texttt{SCHOOL}_i + \alpha_2 \texttt{AGE}_i + \alpha_3 \texttt{Worker}_i \\ &+ \alpha_4 \texttt{EMPLOYEE}_i + \varepsilon_i\end{aligned}$$

In equation (ii), α_4 and α_5 are to be interpreted as the effects of the employment relationships worker or employee relative to the status "civil servant" (holding age and education constant).

2.9.2 (a) The expected income for *men with a high school diploma* is

$$E(Wage|DSEX = 0, DABI = 1) = 3852.73 + 2163.30 = 6016.03\,,$$

while the expected average income for *women with a high school diploma* is estimated by

$$\begin{aligned}&E(Wage|DSEX = 1, DABI = 1) \\ &\qquad = 3852.73 + 2163.30 - 1809.48 - 1074.17 = 3132.38\end{aligned}$$

Note that for women, the interaction term also had to be taken into account. The expected average income for *men without a high school diploma* is estimated as

$$E(Wage|DSEX = 0, DABI = 0) = 3852.73$$

whereas the expected average income for *women without a high school diploma* is

$$E(Wage|DSEX = 1, DABI = 0) = 3852.73 - 1809.48 = 2043.25$$

(b) The interaction term indicates by how much the estimated high school diploma effect differs between men and women. Accordingly, the positive income effect of a high school diploma for women is on average estimated to be 1074.17 euros lower than for their male counterparts.

(c) The average wage of women and men can be calculated using the results from part (a). Thus, the average wage of women is $2043.25 \cdot (1 - 0.4) + 3132.38 \cdot 0.4 = 2478.90$ euros. The average wage of men is $3852.73 \cdot (1 - 0.1) + 6016.03 \cdot 0.1 = 4049.06$ euros. In the total population, men would therefore, despite the assumption of a significantly lower high school diploma rate of 10% (as compared to 40% for females), on average earn more than women.

2.9.3 Considering the results of the ordinary least squares estimation for the complete observation period of 61 years, the estimated model can be written as follows:

$$\widehat{C}_t = 2.0424 + 0.8857 \cdot Y_t^v + 1.8942 \cdot D91_t + 0.0005 \cdot D91_t \cdot Y_t^v$$
$$= (2.0424 + 1.8942 \cdot D91_t) + (0.8857 + 0.0005 \cdot D91_t) \cdot Y_t^v ,$$

where C_t denotes private consumption and Y_t^v disposable income, each at time t. The dummy variable $D91_t$ (value 0 until 1990.4, 1 from 1991.1) introduced into the regression equation is intended to model a possible structural break in the consumption behavior of Germans after reunification, which may have affected both autonomous consumption and the marginal propensity to consume.
Assuming that residual tests show that the requirements imposed on the error terms ε_t are met, the estimated coefficients can be interpreted as follows:

(a) It is evident that an estimation of the consumption function using only West German quarterly data (i.e. $D91_t = 0$) yields a marginal propensity to consume of 88.6%.

(b) The propensity to consume increased by almost 0.05 percentage points after reunification ($D91_t = 1$). For the last almost 30 years of the sample, this results in a marginal propensity to consume for all of Germany of approximately $100 \cdot [\widehat{\beta_2} + \widehat{\beta_4}] = 100 \cdot [0.8857 + 0.0005] = 89.1\%$.

(c) The t-statistics and p-values of the coefficient estimators, also reported in the estimation output, allow the following inference statement in particular: The estimated value for β_4 is, by itself, not significantly different from zero. Since its associated p-value is greater than a chosen significance level of $\alpha = 0.05$, the null hypothesis of long-term stability of income-dependent consumption (H_0: $\beta_4 = 0$) cannot be rejected. The marginal propensity to consume after reunification is therefore not statistically significant different from that previously observed in West Germany. It is thus not necessary to model a structural break in the parameters of the consumption function.
In the years immediately after reunification, partly significant changes in the marginal propensity to consume were observed. These may have been caused by other variables not considered in the model, such as wealth, income distribution, or interest rates, or by different consumption patterns in the new federal states. However, the influence of these factors has apparently weakened so much over time that, for the entire period since reunification, no statistically significant change in the marginal propensity to consume can be identified.

2.9.4 You can find explanations of the linear probability model, including examples, in many introductory textbooks on economics. A key advantage over other estimation methods is that estimated coefficients can be interpreted directly as marginal effects on the probability of the outcome 1. However, when using the linear probability model, the following three problems in particular often occur:

(a) The values predicted by the model, which are interpreted as probabilities for the outcome 1, do not necessarily lie in the interval [0, 1] or [0%, 100%].

(b) The linear probability model exhibits heteroskedastic error terms. However, this can be addressed by using heteroskedasticity-consistent standard errors or by applying weighted least squares estimation.
(c) The error terms are not normally distributed.

2.9.5 No sample solution.

2.9.6 (a) The probability for $\texttt{ABITUR}_i = 1$ is estimated given the values for the explanatory variable $\texttt{GENDER}_i$. It is assumed that there is a latent variable A_i^* ("propensity to obtain the Abitur") that can be modeled linearly, that is:

$$A_i^* = \beta_1 + \beta_2 \texttt{GENDER}_i + \varepsilon_i \, .$$

The link between the unobservable variable A_i^* and the observed realizations is established by assuming that if an unknown threshold value c is exceeded, the outcome is $A_i = 1$, and otherwise $A_i = 0$.

$$\texttt{ABITUR}_i = \begin{cases} 1, & \text{if } A_i^* > c \\ 0, & \text{if } A_i^* \leq c \end{cases}$$

Accordingly, the coefficients β_1 and β_2 as well as the variance of ε_i (σ^2) need to be determined. The probability of having the Abitur can be calculated as follows:

$$\begin{aligned} \text{Prob}(\texttt{ABITUR}_i = 1 | \texttt{GENDER}_i) &= \text{Prob}(A_i^* > c | \texttt{GENDER}_i) \\ &= \text{Prob}(\varepsilon_i > ((c - \beta_1) - \beta_2 \texttt{GENDER}_i)) \, . \end{aligned}$$

Under the usual assumption that the error terms (ε_i) are normally distributed with mean 0 and variance σ^2, it follows that:

$$\text{Prob}(\texttt{ABITUR}_i = 1 | \texttt{GENDER}_i) = \underbrace{\Phi\left(\frac{\beta_1 + \beta_2 \texttt{GENDER}_i}{\sigma}\right)}_{\text{standard normal distribution}}$$

(b) The women in the sample ($\texttt{GENDER} = 1$) have a lower probability of holding the Abitur than men. The hypothesis $\beta_2 = 0$ can be (asymptotically) rejected at the 1% level, since the Z-statistic has a value of -11.235 (this value must be compared with the critical value of the standard normal distribution). The effect of gender on educational attainment is therefore significantly different from zero. A direct interpretation of the size of the coefficients, as in the linear regression model, is not possible. For this, the marginal effects must be calculated, i.e., the partial derivatives of the conditional probability $\text{Prob}(\texttt{ABITUR}_i | \texttt{GENDER}_i)$ with respect to the explanatory variables. These values usually differ from observation to observation. Therefore, the mean of the marginal effects across all observations is often reported.

(c) Instead of the normal distribution, a logistic distribution is assumed for ε.

2.9.7 When interpreting the results, it should be noted that the table does not report the estimated parameters in the Probit model, but rather the resulting marginal effects at the mean of all explanatory variables.

(a) From the positive marginal effect of the dummy `Male`, it can be directly concluded that Italian men, ceteris paribus, have a higher probability of investing in risky financial market assets than women. The effect is statistically significant at the 1% level.

(b) The significantly positive marginal effect of the logarithm of income on the dependent variable `Risky` shows that individuals living in Italy with higher logged income have a higher probability of having invested in risky financial market assets. A 1% increase in income (corresponding to a change in `ln(Income)` of 0.01) thus increases the probability of investing in risky financial assets by $0.117 \cdot 0.01 = 0.0017$, i.e., by 0.0117%.

(c) The marginal effects increase with higher wealth quartiles. The marginal effect for `II Wealth quartile` is not significantly different from zero. Thus, the probability of investing in risky assets does not differ significantly between the 1st and 2nd quartiles of the wealth distribution. Belonging to the 3rd or 4th quartile, however, ceteris paribus, increases the probability of investing in risky financial market assets substantially and statistically significantly relative to the base category, i.e., those with the lowest wealth.

2.9.8 The statement is not correct in its present form. In the linear probability model, the coefficients can be directly interpreted as partial derivatives of the conditional probability $\text{Prob}(D_i|X_i)$ with respect to the explanatory variables and thus as marginal effects.

In contrast, in a Probit model (and likewise in a Logit model), only the signs of the coefficients can be interpreted as in the case of the linear probability model (i.e., the OLS estimation).

Starting from the model for the latent variable: $D_i^* = \beta_1 + \beta_2 X_i + \varepsilon_i$, the marginal effect on the probability that $D_i = 1$ holds can be calculated in the Probit model as follows:

$$\frac{\partial Prob(D_i = 1|X_i)}{\partial X_i} = \frac{\partial \Phi(\beta_1 + \beta_2 X_i)}{\partial X_i} = \phi(\boldsymbol{\beta}_1 + \beta_2 X_i \boldsymbol{\beta}) \cdot \beta_i \,,$$

where Φ denotes the cumulative distribution function and ϕ the density function of the standard normal distribution.

2.9.9 (a) The coefficient of the variable `Gross margin` has a negative sign. Accordingly, the effect of gross margin on the probability of a product being listed is negative.

This does not correspond to the theoretical consideration that a product with a higher gross margin should have an increased chance of being included in the retailer's listings.

To determine whether the effect is significantly different from zero, the reported χ^2 statistic is considered. Converted, this would yield a t-statistic of $\sqrt{10.30} = 3.21$. This value is, in absolute terms, greater than the critical value at the 5% level of 1.96. The null hypothesis that the variable has no effect is therefore rejected at the 5% level. The effect of gross margin on the probability of listing is thus statistically significant different from zero.

(b) From the results, it cannot be directly inferred by how many percentage points the probability of a product being listed increases when the gross margin is doubled, since the model in question is a Logit model. The given coefficients of this model cannot be directly interpreted as in the linear probability model. First, the marginal effect would have to be calculated, which also depends on the values of all other variables for a given observation.

(c) In the table, the diagonal entries represent the number of correct model predictions: the top-left shows 125 products for which the model predicts inclusion and which are actually included, while the bottom-right shows 413 products for which the model predicts no inclusion and which are indeed not included. The other two entries, 98 and 51, therefore represent incorrect predictions. The model would provide a perfect description if these two off-diagonal cells each contained a zero.

5.10 Trend and Seasonal Adjustment

2.10.1 HP-Filter

(a) The formula presented essentially consists of two parts: the first part $\sum_{t=1}^{T}(X_t - H_t)^2$ penalizes deviations of the smoothed component H_t, determined by the HP filter, from the time series X_t under consideration. If the second part of the formula is neglected, the optimal value of the smoothed component at each point in time would simply be the value of the original time series itself, since in that case, the difference between both values would be zero at every time point. The expression shown in the formula would thus be minimized. However, a "filter" that exactly matches the original time series provides no informational gain. Therefore, the second part of the formula

$$\lambda \sum_{t=2}^{T-1} [(H_{t+1} - H_t) - (H_t - H_{t-1})]^2$$

provides smoothing of the component estimated by the HP filter. The smoother the trend path, however, the larger the deviation of the filter from the time series under consideration generally becomes. This illustrates the HP filter's characteristic trade-off between a good fit to the time series and smoothing of the trend. This trade-off leads to a trend path that appears "hand-drawn".

The weight placed on smoothing the filter relative to fitting it can be calibrated using the parameter λ. A low value implies little weight on the smoothing component and thus a strong fit to the time series. For $\lambda = 0$, the second part of the formula disappears, and the path of the smoothed component of the HP filter corresponds exactly to that of the original time series. As λ increases, the path of the filter becomes smoother. In the extreme case $\lambda \to \infty$, the trend path becomes a straight line.

(b) The path of the trend determined by the HP filter at the current edge can change significantly when new values of the time series become available. This reduces the reliability of statements in empirical work that are based on the trend's development. This issue is illustrated in the following small example:

The HP filter is often used to determine the trend or potential output of an economy. This is done by filtering the original gross domestic product (GDP) time series. If the actual GDP in a given year lies above the trend, this is interpreted as a sign of a good economic situation; in the opposite case, it is assumed that the economy is underutilized. Now suppose that the trend path is initially calculated on the basis of GDP data from period t_0 to period t_n in order to draw conclusions about the state of the economy in t_n. Possibly, the actual GDP in t_n lies below the trend path, leading one to conclude an underutilization of the economy in t_n. Subsequently, the GDP value for period t_{n+1} becomes available, and in this example, it is assumed to show a sharp decline compared to t_n. The trend path is then recalculated with this new data point. The poor economic performance in t_{n+1} pulls the trend downward at the current edge. This may cause the actual GDP in t_n to suddenly lie not below but above the trend path. Based on the HP filter, one would now conclude that the economy was in a positive state in t_n, making the earlier assessment of underutilization in t_n obsolete. This example shows how the endpoint problem can cause considerable uncertainty in statements based on the HP filter at the current edge.

2.10.2 (a) The assumption of an additive relationship for decomposing a time series is reasonable when the seasonal fluctuations appear independent of the trend development. A multiplicative relationship, on the other hand, is more appropriate when seasonal and cyclical fluctuations are proportional to the level of the series. For disposable income, a proportional relationship is more likely than a constant amplitude of fluctuations. Therefore, a multiplicative decomposition of the time series is preferable.

(b) Implementation is possible by taking the logarithm of the time series. This transforms the multiplicative (non-linear) model into an additive (linear) one:

$$Y_t^{\text{disp}} = \log(T_t) + \log(Z_t) + \log(S_t) + \log(\varepsilon_t)$$

where $\log(\varepsilon_t)$ can be replaced by u_t.

(c) A component decomposition assumes that a time series can be broken down into trend, cycle, seasonal, and irregular components. However, this is purely a modeling assumption that cannot always be theoretically well justified.

2.10.3 (a) The seasonal component $s_{M,t}$ of a time series y_t can, depending on the data frequency, be decomposed into 2 (semi-annual data), 4 (quarterly data), or 12 (monthly data) components. It is also possible to choose even shorter frequencies, e.g., weeks, days.

Under the assumption of an additive decomposition, the monthly time series X_t can be modeled as

$$y_t = \alpha_1 S_{1,t} + \alpha_2 S_{2,t} + \cdots + \alpha_{12} S_{12,t} + \varepsilon_t\ ,$$

where $S_{M,t}$ denotes a seasonal dummy that takes the value 1 in month M and 0 otherwise. Then, the seasonal component is estimated by

$$\hat{S}_t = \hat{\alpha}_1 S_{1t} + \hat{\alpha}_2 S_{2t} + \cdots + \hat{\alpha}_{12} S_{12t} = \sum_{i=1}^{12} \hat{\alpha}_i S_{it}$$

To avoid perfect multicollinearity in the estimation, either no constant should be included, or one seasonal dummy must be omitted (the constant included in this case would reflect the average of the variable y in the first month if $S_{1,t}$ was omitted).

(b) The reported t-statistics, calculated as

$$t = \frac{\hat{\alpha}_M - 0}{\text{s.e.}\left(\hat{\alpha}_M\right)}$$

are all significantly different from 0 at all critical levels, so that $H_0 : \hat{\alpha}_M = 0$ must be rejected. The average values of y_t therefore differ significantly from zero in each month. However, this does not indicate the relevance of seasonal effects, as it would need to be tested whether the estimated parameters $\hat{\alpha}_M$ differ from one another. This could, for example, be done using an F-test for the null hypothesis $\alpha_1 = \alpha_2, \alpha_1 = \alpha_3, \ldots, \alpha_1 = \alpha_{12}$ (i.e., "no seasonal effects").

(c) The model's forecast reproduces the actual data only moderately accurately (as also suggested by the low R^2 of 0.36). Although no regular seasonal fluctuations appear in the residuals (meaning that seasonal adjustment can be considered successful), some patterns can still be discerned, as the fluctuations of the residuals around zero do not appear entirely random. Further tests are therefore necessary (e.g., DW test for autocorrelation of residuals) to assess the quality of the estimation and the validity of the t-test.

2.10.4 (a) The use of annual growth rates has the advantage of eliminating seasonal effects without having to determine the seasonal component directly. The calculation of continuous annual returns thus allows a comparison of the same months. However, this is results in a loss of information about short-term changes in the time series.

(b) Due to the chosen econometric modeling for these data, one must expect biased t-statistics, as there is an overlap of intervals. In estimation, the problem arises that observations of the original variables s_t and s_{t-1} appear multiple times. This leads to an underestimation of the estimation uncertainty. Thus, the "apparent" seasonal adjustment in this variant may result in faulty inference, i.e., the null hypothesis of no effect of an explanatory variable (in this specific case, past returns) is rejected too often, even though it is true.

(c) The present estimation with monthly returns is preferable to the regression from part b.), as the risk of faulty inference is lower. The result that there is no significant dependence is also more plausible from an economic perspective, since clear dependencies in monthly returns could be profitably exploited by investors in the stock market.

2.10.5 (a) Estimate based on the moving averages of order n

$$Y_t^{\phi n} = \alpha_0 + \alpha_1 X_t^{\phi n} + \varepsilon$$

with

$$Y_t^{\phi n} = \frac{1}{2k+1}\left(Y_{t-k} + \cdots + Y_{t+k}\right)$$

for odd n and

$$Y_t^{\phi n} = \frac{1}{2k}\left(\frac{1}{2}Y_{t-k} + Y_{t-k+1} + \cdots + Y_{t+k-1} + \frac{1}{2}Y_{t+k}\right)$$

for even n (accordingly, the moving average for the time series X_t is also determined). The advantage of this method is its simple implementation. However, at both the beginning and the end, k observations are lost, which are needed for the calculation of the moving averages. Seasonal effects are only smoothed by the procedure, but not completely eliminated. At the same time, moving averages also "blur" cyclical components. In estimation, the problem arises that individual observations of the original variables Y_t and X_t appear in several observations of the moving averages. This leads to an underestimation of the estimation uncertainty and thus tends to produce excessively high t-statistics.

(b) In this case, the estimation is also conducted in two steps. In the first step, the HP-filtered data are calculated. This is done by solving the minimization problem

$$\min[(Y_t - HP_t^y)^2 + \lambda\{(HP_{t+1}^y - HP_t^y) - (HP_t^y - HP_{t-1}^y)\}^2$$

Accordingly, HP_t^x is also calculated. The weighting term λ is chosen depending on data frequency and/or "smoothing preference" (the higher λ, the greater the weight on the latter term and thus the stronger the smoothing of the generated HP_t time series).
In the second step, the generated time series are regressed on each other, i.e.,

$$\mathrm{HP}_t^y = \beta_o + \beta_1 \mathrm{HP}_t^x + \nu_t$$

The advantage of the HP approach is its flexibility regarding one's own adjustment preference. The user can freely choose between an exact representation of the data or the smoothest possible trend component (in the extreme case, a linear course if $\lambda \rightarrow \infty$ is chosen). Moreover, unlike the moving average method, no observations at the edges of the sample are lost. As with the moving average methodology, there is a risk of spurious regression with the HP filter (measuring a relationship that does not actually exist), since the generated data themselves no longer follow an independent stochastic process as required by the OLS method. As a result, the usual distributional assumptions for t- and F-tests no longer hold, which can lead to erroneous conclusions from the significance tests.

(c) Seasonal dummies explicitly measure the seasonal effect (instead of merely smoothing it) and are therefore preferable in the analysis of *constant* seasonal patterns. These can be included in the regression equation. If the data at hand are, for example, quarterly data, the regression would take the following form

$$Y_t = \beta_1 S_{1t} + \beta_2 S_{2t} + \beta_3 S_{3t} + y_4 S_{4t} + \beta_5 X_t + \omega_t$$

where S_{it} captures the individual quarters. In this method, which has the advantage of explicitly quantifying the individual seasonal effects, care must be taken when formulating the regression equation to either include all necessary seasonal dummies or substitute one dummy with the constant, otherwise exact multicollinearity will occur.
A possible disadvantage of the method is that it assumes a constant seasonal pattern.

5.11 Dynamic Models

2.11.1 In general, four arguments can be made that make dynamic modeling appear reasonable or necessary:

1. It is not the current value of a variable, but its development over time that is relevant for a decision.
2. Many economic variables are subject to adjustment inertia.
3. Expectations about the temporal development of a variable are often more decisive than its actual realization.
4. Persistence or hysteresis.

In many economic issues, it is therefore appropriate to explicitly take dynamic aspects into account in modeling. In the simplest case, this is done by considering only the current and lagged values of the explanatory variables:

$$Y_t = \beta_0 + \sum_{k=1}^{\infty} \beta_k X_{t-k+1} \varepsilon_t$$

From such a model, both the short-term and the long-term impact of a change in the explanatory variables can be determined. However, problems arise in practical implementation, since for large k no observations for X_{t-k} are available. One possibility to limit the number of parameters in this context is the use of information criteria.

2.11.2 The starting point is the ADL(1,1) model $Y_t = \alpha_0 + \alpha_1 Y_{t-1} + \beta_0 X_t + \beta_1 X_{t-1} + \varepsilon_t$. With the definitions $\Delta Y_t = Y_t - Y_{t-1}$ and $\Delta X_t = X_t - X_{t-1}$ we obtain

$$\Delta Y_t + Y_{t-1} = \alpha_0 + \alpha_1 Y_{t-1} + \beta_0(\Delta X_t + X_{t-1}) + \beta_1 X_{t-1} + \varepsilon_t \,.$$

Shifting Y_{t-1} to the right (subtracting Y_{t-1} from both sides), combining terms, and factoring out the error correction term yields:

$$\begin{aligned}\Delta Y_t &= \alpha_0 + (\alpha_1 - 1)Y_{t-1} + (\beta_0 + \beta_1)X_{t-1} + \beta_0 \Delta X_t + \varepsilon_t \\ &= \alpha_0 + \beta_0 \Delta X_t - \underbrace{\lambda}_{(1-\alpha_1)} (Y_{t-1} - \underbrace{\gamma}_{\frac{\beta_0+\beta_1}{1-\alpha_1}} X_{t-1}) + \varepsilon_t\end{aligned}$$

2.11.3 (a) This is an error correction model.

(b) An error correction model of the following form was estimated:

$$\begin{aligned}\Delta C_t = \; & \beta_0 + \beta_1 \cdot \Delta Y_t^v - \gamma \cdot (C_{t-1} - \alpha_1 \cdot Y_{t-1}^v) + \beta_2 \cdot SD_1 \\ & + \beta_3 \cdot SD_2 + \beta_4 \cdot SD_3 + \varepsilon_t\end{aligned}$$

$$= \beta_0 + \beta_1 \cdot \Delta Y_t^v - \gamma \cdot C_{t-1} + \gamma \cdot \alpha_1 \cdot Y_{t-1}^v + \beta_2 \cdot SD_1$$
$$+ \beta_3 \cdot SD_2 + \beta_4 \cdot SD_3 + \varepsilon_t$$

(c) The listed coefficients therefore represent

- the direct, short-term effect of changes in income on private consumption (β_1).
- minus the responsiveness of private consumption to deviations from the long-run equilibrium ($-\gamma$).
- the product of responsiveness and the long-run marginal propensity to consume ($\gamma \cdot \alpha_1$)

(d) The long-run marginal propensity to consume is calculated by dividing the coefficient for Y_{t-1}^v by the adjustment coefficient γ, i.e.

$$\alpha_1 = \frac{0.2982}{-(-0.3333)}$$
$$= 0.8947$$

(e) Since this is the ratio of two estimated coefficients, the standard deviation of the long run marginal propensity to consume cannot be obtained from the estimation output directly. Therefore, hypothesis tests for this estimate cannot be carried out using classical methods.

(f) Since the parameter of short-term adjustment (β_1) is larger than that of the long-run equilibrium (α_1), adjustment to the long-run equilibrium state occurs after overshooting in the first period. In the shock period, consumption is adjusted immediately, i.e., in the same period, because $\beta_1 > 0$. However, consumption reaches a level above the long-run solution. This difference is then adjusted in subsequent periods by the share γ of the remaining deviation from the long-run solution. Figure 5.1 illustrates this adjustment dynamic.

5.12 Non-Stationarity and Cointegration

2.12.1 A stochastic process y_t is called strictly stationary if the joint distribution of $(Y_t, Y_{t+1}, Y_{t+2}, \ldots, Y_{t+h})$ is time-invariant for every integer h, i.e., it depends only on the lag h between two observations, but not on the observation time t. If only the first and second moments of the distribution are required to be time-invariant, one arrives at the concept of covariance stationarity.

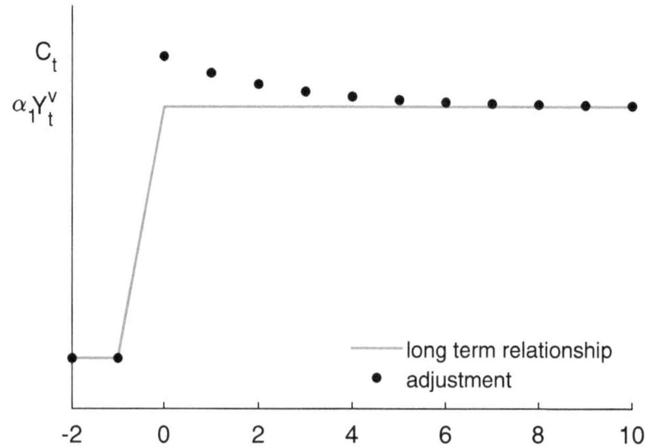

Fig. 5.1 Adjustment dynamics in the error correction model

The process y_t is called weakly stationary or covariance-stationary if its first and second moments remain constant over time. This particularly implies that the expectation, variance, and (auto-)covariances of the process are time-invariant, meaning that:

(i) $E(y_t) \;= \mu_y \qquad\qquad\qquad\qquad \forall\, t \in T$

(ii) $E[(y_t - \mu_y)(y_{t-h} - \mu_y)] \;= \gamma_h \qquad \forall\, t \in T \;\wedge\; h : (t-h) \in T$

This is the commonly used practical definition of stationarity. Accordingly, a time series underlying a stationary stochastic process must fluctuate around a constant mean, which excludes, for example, trending behavior. Moreover, the variance of the time series, i.e. $E[(y_t - \mu_y)^2] = \gamma_0$, must be independent of time t, which also applies to its autocovariances γ_h, which may only depend on the temporal lag h between two observations.

A subgroup of nonstationary processes, i.e., those that do not simultaneously satisfy the above two assumptions, are the so-called *trend-stationary* processes. Their name derives from the fact that they can be transformed into a stationary process by subtracting a deterministic trend (such as the linear trend function $\alpha_0 + \alpha_1 t$ with constant values for α_0 and α_1).

2.12.2 No solution provided.

2.12.3 A spurious regression occurs when a statistically significant relationship is found in the regression of two nonstationary time series, although the variables are actually completely independent of each other. Such errors of type I always appear in statistical tests with a certain probability controlled by the significance level. Commonly, $\alpha = 0.05$ is considered tolerable. However, for regressions with nonstationary time series, the probability of type 1 errors might increases to very high values if standard procedures for stationary time series are used.

Despite the risk of spurious regressions, there can of course also exist genuine relationships between nonstationary time series. This must be checked by appropriate methods (keyword: cointegration).

2.12.4 No solution provided.

2.12.5 A cointegration relationship between two nonstationary time series exists if both considered time series share a similar stochastic trend such that a linear combination of the two variables can be found in which these trends cancel each other out. If such a relationship exists, the variables are said to be cointegrated and one speaks of cointegration.

2.12.6 The Engle-Granger procedure allows testing whether a cointegration relationship exists between two nonstationary variables. The basic approach is carried out in three steps:

1. First, both variables must be tested for stationarity. This is done, for example, using the ADF or KPSS test. Here, three different cases can be distinguished:

   - If only stationary variables are present, the model can be estimated in levels.
   - If, in addition to stationary variables, trend-stationary variables are present, the regression in levels is performed including a deterministic trend.
   - If only nonstationary ($I(1)$) variables are present, these can be used in the second step of the Engle-Granger procedure if they share the same order of integration.

2. Next, the long-run relationship is estimated with OLS. The residuals of this regression $\widehat{\varepsilon}_t$ correspond, as a linear combination of the model variables, to the assumed cointegration relationship.
3. Finally, the stationarity of these residuals is tested using the ADF test. The null hypothesis in this case is "the residuals are nonstationary" or equivalently "no cointegration relationship exists" (Note: since the residuals are not realizations of a stochastic process but calculated results, the usual critical values for the ADF test are not valid).

2.12.7 No solution provided.

5.13 Diagnostics and Forecasting

2.13.1 Economic Policy Simulations:

(a) Starting from the model specification $Y_t = f(X_t) + \varepsilon_t$, a so-called "base solution" or "base simulation" can first be performed, which describes how Y_t behaves given values of X_t, when the error terms ε_t are set to their expected value of zero and the unknown true relationship $f(\cdot)$ is replaced by an estimated function $\hat{f}(\cdot)$:

$$Y_t^b = \hat{f}(X_t)$$

By changing X_t by ΔX_{t0} at time t_0, a simulated path for Y_t results as

$$Y_t^s = \hat{f}(X_t + \Delta X_{t0}) .$$

The simulated effect at t_0 is finally given by the difference of the values for Y_t in the two scenarios, i.e.

$$\Delta Y_0^s = Y_0^s - Y_0^b .$$

(b) **Structural constancy** is the central assumption for the meaningful interpretability of simulations. This means that the functional form of the model, the estimated coefficients, and the distribution of the residuals are time-invariant. This assumption is by no means unproblematic. For example, Robert E. Lucas criticizes econometric models based on static expectations as unrealistic, since there is a constant interaction between economic policy and the decision behavior of market participants. Economic policy measures are taken based on observed decisions of the agents (e.g., an interest rate hike due to positive demand shocks). As intended, these policy measures usually influence the purchasing behavior of the agents. However, the newly made decisions are not necessarily the same as before the economic policy intervention. Thus, the assumption of structural constancy would only be valid to a limited extent.

(c) In Figure 1, a shock causes the new long-term level to be initially overshot. Only over time does the model approach this value. In contrast, in Figure 2, the new level is reached immediately. No dynamic adjustment takes place. While the model used in Figure 1 is apparently **dynamic**, the model in Figure 2 is a **static** model.

(d) This depends on the time perspective. If only the long-term perspective is considered, a static model can be advantageous due to its simpler structure. Usually, however, besides the long-term perspective, the developments on the way there are also important. Then a dynamic modeling approach would be preferable.

(e) Figure (A) $\leftrightarrow$ (2): Figure (A) shows an overshooting adjustment since the new long-term level is only gradually approached from above. For such a course, it must hold that $\beta > \alpha$.

Figure (B) $\leftrightarrow$ (3): This corresponds to the case (A) counterpart. The adjustment "from below" requires that the short-term effect is weaker than the long-term effect, i.e. $\beta < \alpha$.

Figure (C) $\leftrightarrow$ (1): Characteristic for Figure (C) is that no immediate effect occurs. An adjustment only happens with a delay of one period. This is because the short-term effect is zero, i.e. $\beta = 0$.

2.13.2 In the following, Y_t^p denotes the forecast for time t and Y_t the actual realization. Thus, the forecast error can be defined as $e_t = Y_t - Y_t^p$.

(a) The mean forecast error $\overline{e}$ is a measure of the direction and extent of a systematic over- or underestimation. Ideally, this value should be zero, i.e. there should be no systematic over- or underestimation of the forecasts. In the present case, an on average too low forecast is assumed, since $\overline{e} > 0$.

(b) The root mean squared forecast error is defined as follows:

$$RMSE = \sqrt{\frac{1}{T}\sum_{t=1}^{T} e_t^2}$$

The quadratic form gives single large forecast errors much more weight than a large number of small errors. The larger the RMSE, the worse the chosen forecast model. Ideally, the RMSE would be zero.

(c) Using a linear regression model, a systematic bias of the forecasts can be tested.

$$Y_t = \alpha + \beta_1 Y_t^p + \varepsilon_t$$

The null hypothesis $\alpha = 0$ and $\beta_1 = 1$ is tested. If the intercept significantly differs from zero, this would mean that the forecast systematically overestimates ($\alpha < 0$) or underestimates ($\alpha > 0$) the actual values. The null hypothesis $\alpha = 0$ cannot be rejected in the present case. Thus, the forecast does not show a systematic bias.

A value for β_1 greater than one would indicate a conservative forecast, so the predicted changes are on average smaller than the actual ones. The t-statistic can be calculated as follows:

$$t = \frac{\hat{\beta}_1 - 1}{\sqrt{\widehat{V(\hat{\beta}_1)}}} = \frac{0.9931 - 1}{0.0051} = -1.3529$$

At a significance level of $\alpha = 0.05$, the rejection region is

$$[-\infty, -1.96] \cup [1.96, +\infty].$$

Since $t \notin [-\infty, -1.96]$, we **cannot** reject the null hypothesis. Thus, there is no indication of biased forecasts here either. Alternatively, the joint null hypothesis $\alpha = 0$ and $\beta_1 = 1$ could be tested using an F-test.

(d) It is standard in the literature to use a random walk as a naive forecast for price series. This assumes that today's realization is the best possible forecast for tomorrow. Comparing the forecast with futures contracts and this benchmark allows a statement about whether a relative gain in forecasting future realizations is possible.

2.13.3 (a) RMSE stands for "Root Mean Squared Error" and is defined as:

$$RMSE = \sqrt{\frac{1}{T}\sum_{t=1}^{T} e_t^2}$$

where e_t is the forecast error in period t. If all forecast errors are small, so are the squared values e_t^2, thus their sum and its root should also be small. Ideally, all forecast errors are zero and thus the RMSE is zero.

(b) The RMSE is a non-normalized measure of forecast quality, i.e. apart from the minimal value zero, no boundary between good and less good forecasts can be specified. The Theil inequality coefficient U allows a comparison of forecasts and is defined as the ratio of the RMSE of the forecast to be evaluated and an alternative forecast, often called the benchmark forecast, i.e. $U = RMSE_1/RMSE_2$, where $RMSE_1$ in the present case is the RMSE of the SVR forecasts, namely 1.9218, and $RMSE_2$ is the RMSE of the alternative forecasts. A value of U less than one means the forecast considered produces smaller quadratic errors than the benchmark, while a value of U greater than one implies the forecast is worse than the benchmark.
Comparing the SVR forecast with the naive forecast that assumes GDP growth is constantly zero, results in $U_{constant} = 1.9218/2.7313 = 0.7036 < 1$. Thus, SVR forecasts deliver better results for real GDP growth than a naive forecast assuming zero real growth.
Comparing the SVR forecast instead with the forecast that simply continues the previous period's GDP growth, yields $U_{RandomWalk} = 1.9218/1.3956 = 1.3770$. Compared to this alternative benchmark of the random walk, which can also be obtained without much effort, the SVR forecasts perform worse in terms of mean squared error in the considered period.

(c) Since the inflation rate exhibits relatively high persistence, it would be natural to use the previous period's value as a benchmark forecast. This benchmark is certainly harder to outperform than a naive forecast assuming no inflation or using the long-term average inflation in the past. When interpreting statements about forecast quality based on Theil's U, it is always important to consider which benchmark forecast was used.

2.13.4 (a) The ZEW economic sentiment indicator is a leading indicator used for early forecasting of industrial production. It reflects economic expectations in six months. The truck toll performance index is more of a concurrent indicator because the transport performance comprises both intermediate goods for future production and goods for final consumption from past production. Accordingly, the ZEW sentiment indicator would be preferred for medium- and long-term forecasts, while the truck toll performance index, also due to its daily availability, can support a preliminary estimate of industrial production in the current month (keyword: nowcasting).

(b) The estimated coefficient for `ZEWSENT(-6)` is 0.0511 and positive, indicating that higher economic sentiment six months ago is associated with higher growth in industrial production. This is economically plausible, as positive sentiment generally signals expectations of increased production. The R^2 of 0.1536 shows that about 15.36% of the variation in the six-month industrial production growth rate is explained by the variance of the lagged sentiment indicator. However, the Durbin-Watson statistic of 0.53 suggests strong positive autocorrelation in the residuals, indicating a risk of biased standard errors and inference. Therefore, corrections for autocorrelation or time series-specific modeling approaches are recommended.

(c) Although the truck toll performance index shows a significantly positive relationship with industrial production changes, it is fundamentally less suitable for forecasting a six-month horizon. Since it is more of a coincident indicator reflecting transport activity related to both past and current production, it is better used for nowcasting or very short-term forecasts rather than medium-term forecasting.

Solutions for Selected Text-Related Exercises 6

In this chapter, you will find some solutions or hints for some selected text-related exercises presented in Chap. 3. Please note that many questions may not have a single correct answer, e.g., when examples are requested. The sample solutions are intended to help you check your own performance. You should therefore try to solve the questions independently first before consulting the sample solutions. The numbering of the solutions corresponds to the numbering of the questions.

6.1 Tasks and Principles of Empirical Economic Research

3.1.1 Solution hint:

(a) Examples of the tasks of empirical economic research addressed in the first chapter:

- Analysis of past developments: The report notes that Germany's real GDP has grown by only 0.1% in real terms since 2019, with detailed references to sector-specific developments such as declines in mechanical engineering and construction. This is a typical retrospective analysis used to assess economic performance.
- Evaluation of the current situation (diagnosis): The German Council of Economic Experts diagnoses ongoing structural and cyclical problems, such as high uncertainty, rising production costs, and declining competitiveness in manufacturing. This is meant to explain why the recovery has failed to take effect.

P. Winker et al., *Exercise Book Empirical Economic Research and Econometrics*,
https://doi.org/10.1007/978-3-662-72713-3_6

- Conditional forecast: The council projects a decline in real GDP by 0.1% in 2024 and growth of 0.4% in 2025. These forecasts are conditional on certain assumptions, such as developments in the global economy, ECB monetary policy, and geopolitical stability.

(b) Concept of a "conditional forecast" and examples from the text:

- A conditional forecast predicts future developments (e.g., GDP growth) if specific external conditions hold true. It is not an absolute prediction but depends on those conditions being met.
- Conditions from Chart 1 and the text:
  - The global economy grows as projected, at 2.6% in 2024 and 2025.
  - The ECB continues to cut interest rates, stimulating investment and consumption. This is mentioned as a growth stimulant in 2025.
  - Geopolitical risks (Middle East conflict, Ukraine war) do not escalate significantly and energy prices remain stable.
  - German manufacturing output gradually recovers, with no major new declines in exports or investment.
  - The household saving rate remains high or falls only moderately.

  These are assumptions that, if not fulfilled, would likely lead to different GDP outcomes than the stated 0.4% growth forecast for 2025.

3.1.2 (a) Within the framework of the three core tasks discussed in the lecture, the study mainly addresses the task of evaluating the current situation and an alternative policy scenario. Based on German microdata (GSOEP), the authors simulate the expected fiscal and distributional effects of introducing a monthly €2, 000 tax allowance for earnings above the statutory retirement age. They estimate the number of beneficiaries (about 230,000), the initial revenue loss (€770 million per year) and show that higher earners would benefit more. They also forecast alternative scenarios with higher employment among pensioners (+75,000 or +150,000), identifying the thresholds at which the measure could become fiscally neutral or positive. This ex-ante policy simulation is relevant for political decision-making because it provides quantitative projections of costs, distributional impacts, and possible labor supply effects, thereby informing whether the reform should be implemented.

(b) The question cannot be answered solely on the basis of this study. While the authors point out equality considerations in favor of including the self-employed, their simulations also indicate substantially higher fiscal costs (around €1.5 billion per year) and a greater risk of windfall gains, with likely smaller additional employment effects for the self-employed. They further highlight data limitations, notably the under-reporting of self-employment income in the data, and stress the uncertainty surrounding behavioral responses.

As a result, the paper provides useful orientation but no sufficient evidence for a definitive policy decision, which would require better data and causal evidence on labor supply reactions. Even with more robust findings, they could not answer the fairness question of including or not the group of self-employed.

6.2 Data Basis of Empirical Economic Research

3.2.1 (a) Some arguments provided in the article:

- GDP measures only economic output, not overall well-being.
- It does not capture social dimensions such as health, safety, and happiness.
- Inequality and poverty are overlooked (for example, 38% of global wealth growth from 1995–2021 reached the top 1%).
- Focusing on short-term GDP growth can lead to environmental degradation, harming the well-being of future generations.
- Above a certain income level, there is no strong correlation between GDP growth and subjective well-being.

(b) The authors propose a three-dimensional framework for measuring well-being, which includes well-being (current average well-being), inclusion (equitable distribution of well-being), and sustainability (conditions for future well-being). Their approach integrates insights from five scientific traditions: subjective well-being, welfare economics, needs theories, the capabilities approach, and ecological perspectives. Measurement relies on subjective and objective indicators with the aim of creating a standardized but also flexible system that can be adapted to the specific circumstances of different countries.

(c) The authors suggest measuring broader well-being by developing a dashboard of indicators covering the three dimensions mentioned above, such as life expectancy, access to health care, emissions per capita, and voter turnout. Existing indices, including the Human Development Index, the Sustainable Development Goals and the Ecological Footprint, could be incorporated into a structured format. The framework should allow country-specific values and indicators to reflect cultural and economic differences. In the long term, the goal is to establish an international "well-being accounting system", analogous to the System of National Accounts.

3.2.2 (a) FDI is relevant for the financial account (monthly transactions, market value), the international investment position (quarterly stocks), and the FDI stock statistics (annual stocks, book value). A benchmark definition ensures internationally comparable data across the OECD countries.

(b) The Bundesbank measures FDI as cross-border investment that gives lasting influence ($\geq 10\%$ shares/votes; $> 50\% =$ control), following the IMF BPM6[1] and the OECD standards. The threshold 10% is assumed to be a practical and internationally accepted cut-off point.

(c) In long ownership chains, Germany's DIIC method omits some indirectly controlled enterprises included in the OECD benchmark. Applying the benchmark fully would increase the reported German outward FDI.

6.3 Data Processing

3.3.1 (a) Alternative methods include option pricing (for example, adding the cost of specific features such as airbags in cars), judgmental adjustments (expert evaluations of statistical offices, such as efficiency improvements in washing machines), hedonic regression methods (linking product characteristics to price, for example, used for PCs, smartphones, printers, used cars), and quantity adjustments (correcting for package size or number of units). These methods try to isolate the change in "pure price" from changes in quality or product composition.

(a) The authors used German CPI microdata from 2010 to 2020, which provide both raw prices as collected in stores and adjusted prices that enter the official CPI. Adjustments take place in two steps: first, raw prices are corrected for package or unit size changes; second, a quality adjustment variable records price differences when a product is replaced by one of higher or lower quality. Negative values mean improvements, positive values mean deterioration. Aggregation to inflation measures follows the official Destatis procedure, allowing the authors to compare inflation based on raw prices with inflation that accounts for quality and quantity changes.

(c) Quality adjustment has opposite effects depending on the product. For insurance premiums, coverage has worsened over time, so quality adjustment raises the effective price and thus inflation. By contrast, durable goods like cars, washing machines, or televisions have improved in features and efficiency, so quality adjustment reduces their price increases. Inflation therefore rises when quality declines and falls when quality improves.

(d) The authors find that quality adjustments lower average German inflation by about 0.1 percentage points between 2010 and 2020. Without quality adjustment, the inflation would have been slightly higher. However, this is considered a lower bound, because the dataset lacks centrally collected products strongly

[1] Sixth Edition of the IMF's Balance of Payments and International Investment Position Manual: https://www.imf.org/external/pubs/ft/bop/2007/bopman6.htm.

affected by quality changes, such as computers, smartphones, and used cars. When supplementing with scanner data for such goods, the estimated effect increases to around 0.6 percentage points, closer to previous studies for Germany and Sweden.

6.4 Economic Indicators

3.4.1 (a) According to the ECB's Governing Council decision from 1998, price stability is defined as a year-on-year increase in the harmonized consumer price index (HICP) of below 2% over the medium term. One argument for a positive inflation rate mentioned in the text (page 8) is a possible upward bias of the HICP measure of inflation. A number of arguments for the HICP as specific inflation indicator is provided in the second paragraph on page 9. These arguments include the similarity to national consumer price indices, the timely availability, the monthly frequency, and the comparability across euro area countries. Furthermore, it is stated on page 10 that inflation perceptions (from consumer surveys) are in line with the HICP measures.

(b) In order to address some limitations of the original HCPI due to delayed adjustments of baskets and product weights or missing quality adjustments, some changes have been made to the HICP after 2003. For example, prices with high frequency fluctuations (such as fuel) are sampled at several days within a month, seasonal items become more weight in the baskets, and HICP weights are updated annually.

(c) For example, substitution of products by others due to changes in relative prices might lead to biases if not taken into account properly. Also changes in quality of a product, which affect the price, should be taken into account to avoid biases. A further relevant aspect is the inclusion of new products and services.

(d) The cost of owner-occupied housing represents a substantial share of consumers' expenditures. Consequently, changes in these cost have an impact on perceived inflation that is only partially reflected in the HICP in its current version.

The two approaches (NA based on national accounts) and RE (rental equivalence) are described in detail in Sect. 4.2 (p. 51ff) including a set of arguments in favor of one or the other approach.

3.4.2 (a) Since the beginning of 2021, the CPI inflation rate in the G7 countries increased sharply. From around 0.7% in early 2021 they soared to a peak of 8.6% by October 2022, with some countries reaching double-digit inflation during that year. These are the highest inflation rates in these economies since the 1980s.

(b) Three factors the text mentions are:

- Rapid rebound in global demand for goods due to fiscal and monetary stimulus implemented to counteract effects of the pandemic.

- Supply-side bottlenecks, including COVID disruptions, strained logistics, lack empty shipping containers, and port congestion.
- The sharp increase in commodity prices, especially energy and food, intensified by uncertainty following Russia's war of aggression against Ukraine.

(c) With services restricted during the pandemic (e.g., travel, restaurants), consumers shifted spending toward goods. This sudden boom in demand clashed with limited supply capacity, as production had not increased to the same extent and logistics were still constrained. Together, this pushed up prices throughout the value chain, from intermediate inputs to consumer goods.

(d) High demand met diminished supply capacity, pushing input costs higher (e.g., transport, raw materials). Producers, facing higher costs and sustained demand, increased their mark-ups to maintain profits. These elevated mark-ups led to higher prices for consumers.

(e) The war intensified already high commodity price pressures. In particular, energy and food prices spiked sharply after the invasion, driven by uncertainty about Russian supply and difficulties in accessing alternative sources.

3.4.3 (a) The "at-risk-of-poverty rate" is clearly based on a relative concept of poverty. As explained in the report, the threshold is conventionally set at 60% of the median net equivalised income. This means that poverty is measured in relation to the income distribution within the society rather than against a fixed standard of basic needs.

(b) If all incomes doubled, the median income would also double, and therefore the poverty threshold (60% of the median) would double as well. Since each household's relative position in the income distribution would remain unchanged, the at-risk-of-poverty rate itself would remain the same. In other words, because the measure is relative, uniform proportional increases in income do not change the rate.

(c) The material deprivation rate is based on an absolute concept of poverty. It measures the share of people unable to afford a set of specific goods or activities (such as adequate heating, regular meals, or certain durable goods). Since this definition refers to concrete living conditions rather than relative income positions, a general doubling of income would likely reduce the material deprivation rate. More households would be able to afford the listed items, so both material deprivation and severe material deprivation would tend to decline.

6.5 Input-Output Analysis

3.5.1 The article deals with employment effects related to renewable energy in Germany.

(a) In Chap. 2 they state as the main advantage that the Input-Output analysis allows for the consideration of direct effects related to renewable energy investments (and service), as well as of the activities that are indirectly triggered due to input requirements of the production in the investment sector over all stages of production.

(b) The main issue with the Input-Output tables for this purpose is that they have 71 sectors and none of them corresponds one-to-one to the renewable energy industry. To solve this problem, they generate data for 22 new sectors corresponding to renewable energy investment and services. This represents a major challenge described in detail in the article.

(c) The labor coefficients are used to derive the sector-specific labor required to produce one more unit of gross output. Thus, conceptually they belong to the input coefficients not related to intermediate products from the 71 sectors. For the 71 existing sectors, they are available in the Input-Output table. For the new sectors, they are calculated by the authors.

3.5.2 The text addresses direct and indirect effects of the gas price increase at the end of 2021 and the beginning of 2022.

(a) For example, the production of plastic bottles in the sector "Rubber and plastic products" requires polyethylene originating in the sector "Chemical products" The energy used to produce polyethylene represents the indirect energy used, while only the energy used to produce polyethylene bottles is directly attributed to the sector "Rubber and plastic products".

(b) The lack of gas has direct effects on the sectors that use it as a production input, while it also might indirectly affect the production capacities. In the example, the direct effect would lead to a reduction in the machine's capacity to manufacture plastic bottles to run, while the indirect effect could be a lack of polyethylene due to constraints in the sector "Chemical products".

The shock is introduced in the Input-Output model assuming a 10% decrease in the output of the sector "electricity, gas, steam and air conditioning" going as input for all other sectors.

6.6 The Econometric Model

3.6.1 (a) The author mentions two main differences. First, it is difficult to run controlled experiments in economics such that all other possible factors influencing the outcome remain constant. However, since the publication of the article in 1969 there has been a substantial development in experimental economics.

Second, while the laws of classical physics are known and precisely, the economic "laws" are less accurate. Thus, statements about links between some influential factor and the outcome are statistical statements. Therefore, considering the uncertainty surrounding the econometric estimates is quite important.

(b) The central argument is that any economic result will depend not just on a single factor but on many of them. It might be difficult or sometimes even impossible to obtain a measure of all these factors. Therefore, the model can only be an approximation (see footnote 1 in the article).

(c) In an experimental setting, we would have to control for the influence of possibly many factors, which is not feasible with limited resources. In the econometric model, it is possible to measure the impact of all these factors together.

(d) Applications discussed include forecasting, e.g. of prices, but also evaluation of policy measures such as a devaluation of the currency or the introduction of a tax on consumers.

6.7 The Linear Regression Model

3.7.1 (a) The specification starts with a standard supply function linking the logarithm of output to the logarithm of real prices. In this functional specification, a log-log model, the coefficient for the explanatory variable (labeled γ in the application) can be interpreted as elasticity, i.e., it measures by how many percent the output will change as a reaction to a one percent increase in prices. The author augments this basic specification by a linear trend term that is assumed to reflect structural changes of the oil market, e.g. due to the increasing relevance of non-OECD suppliers.

(b) The result for the OPEC aggregate can be found in the line beginning with OPEC. The estimated relationship is:

$$ln Q_t^{OPEC} = 16.81 - 0.169 ln P_t - 0.003t + \hat{\varepsilon}_t$$

This results implies that an increase of the prices by 1% would decrease the total production of OPEC by 0.169%.

(c) The result of the estimation for the non-OPEC countries is:

$$ln Q_t^{non-OPEC} = -15.79 + 0.106 ln P_t + 0.103t + \hat{\varepsilon}_t$$

In this case, a price increase by 1% leads to an expected increase in supply by 0. 106%.

(d) The author argues that the OPEC countries might follow a target revenu strategy, while the non-OPEC countries behave more according to the competitive hypothesis.

(e) No solution provided. You might consider the relatively low R^2 for OPEC countries and think about variables that might be missing. You can also discuss whether the assumed linear trend is appropriate and which properties you would expect for the residuals of the estimated equations.

6.8 Qualitative Variables

3.8.1 (a) The ordered probit model is more appropriate because the dependent variable is categorical and ordinal, not continuous. Linear regression can predict impossible values outside the categories and violates assumptions like homoscedasticity and normality of errors. The ordered probit explicitly models category probabilities based on an underlying latent variable, making it suitable for discrete outcomes.

(b) The thresholds τ_1 and τ_2 divide the latent continuous variable into intervals corresponding to each observed category: below τ_1 means a rate decrease, between τ_1 and τ_2 means no change, and above τ_2 means a rate increase. These thresholds determine the probability ranges for each interest rate decision by mapping the latent variable to discrete outcomes via the cumulative normal distribution.

(c) A positive coefficient β on the ECB Communication Stance Indicator (CI) implies that an increase in CI increases the value of the latent variable, shifting the probability to higher categories. This increases the likelihood of an interest rate increase (+1) and decreases the chance of a cut ($-$ 1), assuming that all other factors are kept constant.

(d) One-step ahead forecasting uses explanatory variables lagged by one period to predict the interest rate decision of the current. This respects the timing of information, ensuring that predictions are based only on data available at the forecast time, thus avoiding look-ahead bias.

(e) To examine whether "geopolitical risks" are important, include this variable as an explanatory factor in the ordered probit model and estimate the model using maximum likelihood. If the estimated coefficient for "geopolitical risks" is significantly different from zero, this suggests that it has an influence. You could also look at whether adding this variable improves the fit of the model (for example, by increasing the pseudo R^2), which would further indicate that it helps explain interest rate decisions.

6.9 Trend and Seasonal Adjustment

3.9.1 (a) Capacity utilization is used as a measure of demand side pressure, which is assumed to have a potential impact on the development of producer prices and, consequently, on inflation.

(b) In the short term, high levels of utilization can increase production cost, reduce marginal productivity, and increase profit margins. Thus, prices might increase. Therefore, the indicator might be seen as a leading indicator of inflation.

(c) The survey aims to provide quantitative measures of the current degree of capacity utilization. To this end, the output changes due to different levels of utilization must be separated from the output changes related to the changes in the level of capacities. The text mentions the use of long-term averages or trends in capacities as well as statistical filters to separate the two effects.

(d) Deviations are shown to provide information on the relative degree of pressure on the demand side, independent of long-term developments.

3.9.2 (a) Seasonal adjustment aims to remove recurring seasonal patterns in economic data (e.g. due to holidays, seasonal production in agriculture, or constraints in construction work during winter) to reveal the underlying cyclical and trend components. Therefore, the impact of a typical winter season is eliminated by seasonal adjustment, while the influence of unusual conditions such as very mild winters or heat waves, lack of rain, or unusual long frost periods is still contained in the adjusted data.

(b) First, an indicator of weather effects is selected. The Bundesbank proposed using the number of ice days in a quarter. Next, the GDP quarter-to-quarter growth rate is regressed on the indicator to estimate the weather effect. Finally, the estimated effect is subtracted from the already seasonally adjusted data. Obviously, the number of ice days is not the only relevant weather effect. Thus, residual weather effects such as heat waves exist, which are not taken into account in the proposed procedure.

(c) There are two effects: due to the higher level of GDP in the first quarter, quarter-to-quarter growth rates would be smaller for the second quarter. Second, it depends on whether the activities in the first quarter are just withdrawn from following periods. According to the article, the authors expect that the activities will be additional ones.

3.9.3 (a) One method consists in estimating a linear trend to the logarithm of GDP, which is called a log-linear trend component. The second method is the so-called Hodrick-Prescott filter. You can find a technical description in many textbooks.

(b) The figure shows the issue of extrapolating deterministic trends. The trend estimated for the period 2003–2007 would have indicated an unrealistic expected growth for the years following the financial market crises. In contrast, a trend estimated for the period 2008–2013 would have pointed to almost no growth. Obviously, both trends are not useful in describing the actual development after 2008.

(c) The form of a trend derived from the Hodrick-Prescott filter (HP) depends on all observations. It might change substantially for the most recent period when additional observations become available. Fore example, while the HP trend was seemed to increase steeply by the end of 2007, the estimate including the data until end of 2009 indicated a rather small trend growth for 2007.

The authors suggest that using an econometric model, e.g. based on the production function, might provide more useful trend approximations than purely statistical methods.

(d) GDP data become available only with some delay after the end of the quarter (availability). Furthermore, they are subject to revisions for extended periods as new and more precise data become available for the respective quarter.

6.10 Dynamic Models

3.10.1 (a) The authors argue that bank lending and deposit rates usually follow market interest rates. However, some of the adjustment to changes in market interest rates take place in the short-run, while another part follows with a delay. The error correction model is well suited to reflect both immediate adjustments and convergence to some long-run relationship.

(b) The estimated error correction model is given by

$$\Delta r_t^B = \beta_1 + \beta_2 \Delta r_t^M + \beta_3 r_{t-1}^B + \beta_4 r_{t-1}^M + \varepsilon_t \, .$$

The *Immediate pass-through* is measured by β_2, the *Adjustment speed* corresponds to $beta_3$, and the *Long-term pass-through* is obtained by dividing β_4 by $-\beta_3$. Please note that in the usual presentation of results from an error correction model, the adjustment speed is indicated as $-\beta_3$.

(c) The immediate pass-through is lower than the long-term pass-through. Only for loans to non-financial corporations, it is quite substantial. The long-term pass-through is markedly below one for deposits, while it is closer to but still below one for loans. For differences in the pass-through of loan rates, the authors refer to the long interest rate fixation periods for loans to households for house purchases. Obviously, this reduces the adjustment speed of aggregate interest rates.

6.11 Non-Stationarity and Cointegration

3.11.1 (a) The idea of the Dickey-Fuller approach is to test the null hypothesis of a unit root, i.e. whether the coefficient γ in the model $G_t = \gamma G_{t-1} + \varepsilon_t$ is equal to zero. According to the statements at the top of page 2, second column, this null hypothesis could not be rejected for both variables. Therefore, it is assumed that both time series are nonstationary.

(b) As stated in the paper, when the nonstationarity of the variables is ignored and standard analysis is performed, the results might lead to invalid inference. For example, a standard t-test might indicate that α is differs significantly (in the statistical sense) from zero, while there is no real link between the variables.

(c) One way of dealing with nonstationarity consists in searching for cointegration. The authors used the Engle-Granger approach. It consists of estimating the standard regression and testing the residuals of this regression for nonstationarity using different critical values from the standard Dickey-Fuller test to account for the fact that the residuals are not observed but objective variables. The test leads to a rejection of the null hypothesis of nonstationarity of the residuals. Hence, a cointegration relationship between G_t and E_t is found and can be meaningfully interpreted.

(d) The Jarque-Bera test is a test of the null hypothesis that error terms of a linear regression model are normally distributed. The null hypothesis is not rejected. This implies normality of estimates even in a finite sample. Otherwise, one would have to argue that a large sample implies normality at least asymptotically.

6.12 Diagnostics and Forecasting

3.12.1 (a) Forecasts of medium-term growth are difficult. The forecasts mentioned in the text are either based on a surevy of forecasts from other institutions (consensus economics) or on predictions of major growth components including capital and employment. If past trend forecasts have been overly optimistic or pessimistic, an adjustment of future forecasts could be made by subtracting or adding the mean error of past forecasts.

(b) The growth of per capita output is driven by capital per worker, the participation of the labor force, the employment rate, and the total factor productivity (technology). The decline in growth rates in developed economies is mainly attributed to a lower growth rate of total factor productivity.

3.12.2 (a) Inflation expectations are broadly measured in two ways: survey-based measures and market-based measures. Survey-based approaches directly ask individuals or professional forecasters about their expected inflation, while market-based methods infer expectations from the pricing of financial assets like inflation-linked bonds.

(b) Survey-based measures, such as those from the Survey of Professional Forecasters (SPF), offer direct insight into people's stated beliefs about future inflation. However, they can be prone to bias from the way questions are phrased or if respondents lack strong incentives to provide precise answers.

(c) Market-based measures, such as the 5-year/5-year forward inflation swap rate, are derived from financial market data. They provide aggregated real-time expectations from a wide range of market participants. However, these measures can be influenced by factors beyond pure inflation expectations, such as risk premiums or market liquidity.

(d) Short-term inflation expectations reflect immediate inflation trends, providing insight into near-term price developments. In contrast, long-term inflation expectations serve as a gauge of a central bank's credibility in achieving its inflation target over time. Both are crucial for central banks, as they inform both immediate policy responses and the assessment of long-term policy effectiveness.

MIX
Papier aus verantwortungsvollen Quellen
Paper from responsible sources
FSC® C105338

If you have any concerns about our products,
you can contact us on
ProductSafety@springernature.com

In case Publisher is established outside the EU,
the EU authorized representative is:
Springer Nature Customer Service Center GmbH
Europaplatz 3, 69115 Heidelberg, Germany

Printed by Libri Plureos GmbH
in Hamburg, Germany